10 WEEK BIBLE

1 SAMUEL

10WeekBooks.com

1 SAMUEL: A 10 WEEK BIBLE STUDY

Copyright © 2017 Darren Hibbs
Published by 10 Week Books

All rights reserved.

Scriptures taken from the Holy Bible, New International Version®, NIV®. Copyright © 1973, 1978, 1984, 2011 by Biblica, Inc.™ Used by permission of Zondervan. All rights reserved worldwide. www.zondervan.com   The "NIV" and "New International Version" are trademarks registered in the United States Patent and Trademark Office by Biblica, Inc.™

ISBN-13: 978-0-9997312-7-7

Cover: Saul Attacking David, Guercino 1646 — Public Domain

No part of this book may be reproduced in any form or by any electronic or mechanical means including information storage and retrieval systems, without permission in writing from the author. The only exception is by a reviewer, who may quote short excerpts in a review.

10WeekBooks.com

For Doug & Diana Hibbs

You raised me to know the Lord. What greater a gift can parents give to a son? It is because of your example, your devotion and your love that I am who I am today. I love and appreciate both of you more than words can express.

Contents

About the 10 Week Bible Study....................iii

Introduction To 1 Samuel............................v

Outline of 1 Samuel.......................................vii

1 - 1 Samuel 1-3..2

2 - 1 Samuel 4-6..19

3 - 1 Samuel 7-9..36

4 - 1 Samuel 10-12 55

5 - 1 Samuel 13-15 71

6 - 1 Samuel 16-18 92

7 - 1 Samuel 19-21 112

8 - 1 Samuel 22-24 129

9 - 1 Samuel 25-27 144

10 - 1 Samuel 28-31 159

   Reading Chart...175

   About The Author 176

   Other Titles by 10 Week Bible 177

ABOUT THE 10 WEEK BIBLE STUDY

My heart is to see people fall in love with God through growing in His Word. The 10 Week Bible Study helps people do that through repetition, helpful commentary and engaging questions. Most of all, this study helps people stay engaged by encouraging them to keep going when they get off track, get confused or get lost.

David, in Psalm 1, told us that if we meditated on God's Word day and night, we would be like a tree planted by rivers of living water. I don't know about you, but I find it hard to remember to meditate at all hours of the day. The 10 Week Bible Study makes that easy by encouraging people to read the book of the Bible being studied 10 times in 10 weeks (hence the name).

When you start reading God's Word like that, you'll find that you accidentally meditate on His Word. In those moments when your mind is at rest and blank, it always snaps to something you've been thinking about. When you pull up to the stoplight, maybe your mind goes to work, chores or that show you've been binging on Netflix lately. With the 10 Week Bible Study, you'll find yourself thinking about God's Word in those moments. You may just catch yourself asking God questions about what you've been reading without even thinking about it.

That is what David meant by meditating on God's Word day and night, that your heart and mind are so full of His Word that you can't help but think about it in those quiet times.

ADDITIONAL RESOURCES

Join the growing community of people who listen, watch and discuss the 10 Week Bible Study online. With millions of downloads and thousands of free resources to choose from, the 10 Week Bible Study produces daily podcasts, videos and other downloadable content to help you grow in your walk with God.

For more information and to join our email list to get regular encouragement in God's Word, visit 10Week-Bible.com today.

Introduction To 1 Samuel

The book of 1st Samuel is one of the best books in the Bible for people becoming familiar with God's Word. It is a great book to recommend people to read as a place to start. It is one of the most disarming books of the Bible because it reads like a novel. There is mystery, intrigue, jealousy, murder, anger, strife, infidelity, war, tragedy, comedy, triumph and loss.

The Samuels are the most salacious piece of scripture available to read. They are filled with interesting stories of fallen people trying to interact with their Creator God the best way they can. The conflicts, victories and failures contained within are something that everyone can relate to in one way or another.

Samuel, David and Saul are examples for us even today. Samuel, the great prophetic reformer, can instruct us in the ways God moves when we least expect it. Saul, the tragic leader who never learns to overcome his besetting sins, will show us every way not to relate to the Lord. David, though far from perfect, is our example of what a fallen man who loves the Lord with all his heart can truly be.

First and Second Samuel are actually the same book split into two volumes in our modern Bibles. As a natural breaking point in the narrative, our book will end with tragedy, but fear not, redemption lies just around the corner in 2 Samuel.

Reading 1 Samuel ten times in ten weeks will dramatically increase your experience with the book. There are many things within the book that are not immediately clear until you are thoroughly familiar with the book. The author intended for us to read this book over and over again to gain the insights he included within.

As for authorship, it is actually not Samuel. He may have authored some of the source material for the beginning of the book, or the beginning itself, but he is clearly dead before most of the book happens. We do not know who our author is or exactly when the book was written, but all evidence points to a now anonymous author sometime around or before the exile of the Jews to Babylon.

The book not being authored close to the events does not take away from the fact that it is indeed scripture. We can understand that the events contained in this book are a "Reader's Digest", or condensed version, of the events, but that these retellings of the stories were the ones the Lord wanted included in the Canon of Scripture the way He wanted them told.

1 Samuel will challenge you, inspire you and draw you closer to the God who loves and relates to very fallen people. People like you and me.

OUTLINE OF 1 SAMUEL

Chapters 1-7
    All About Samuel

Chapters 8-13:15
    Transition to a Kingdom

Chapters 13:16-15:35
    The Tragedy of Saul

Chapters 16-17
    Introducing David

Chapters 18-27
    David's Dark Days (Or Israel's Dark Days)

Chapters 28 & 31
    The Demise of Saul

Chapters 29-30
    The End of David's Darkness

1 Samuel in 10 Weeks

1 Samuel 1-3

Study Questions

1. What tribe was Samuel from?

2. Who wrote 1 Samuel and when?

3. Why was Hannah so upset about not having children? What was a time you felt like Hannah, and how did you respond?

WEEK 1 | 1 SAMUEL 1 - 3

4. Why did Eli think Hannah was drunk?

5. What was so wrong about what Hophni and Phinehas were doing?

6. Why did the Lord speak so harshly to Eli through the nameless prophet? Do you think the Lord would still speak to us like that today? Why and when would He speak to us like that?

7. What, according to our author, does it mean to "know the Lord" as Samuel did?

COMMENTARY NOTES

INTRODUCTION

1 Samuel is an encouraging and happy journey for anyone reading or studying the Bible. It is an exciting story, narrated from the perspective of hindsight so that we can fully engage in what God is doing with the history of Israel.

AUTHOR AND DATE

Despite the name of the book, no one actually knows who wrote 1st and 2nd Samuel. In the Hebrew Bible they are one book, separated in the Christian Bible for the sake of length.

Samuel could not have written most of the book because he dies in chapter 25 of 1 Samuel. Many scholars believe that Samuel was compiled and rewritten from multiple source texts, possibly from Samuel himself as well as the prophets Nathan and Gad.

Being written from source texts makes this work no less scripture than anything else and no less inspired by God. There were many books written that were later either lost or compiled into books such as Samuel, Kings and Chronicles. These books span multiple generations, but contain details of stories that seem to be the work of excellent historians using the inspired words of the original authors themselves.

There are many clues in the book as to when it was

written in full. Many statements allude to the fact that it is looking back hundreds of years, like when we are told that Ziklag has belonged to "the kings of Judah to this day." What is this day? It is a day after the kingdom of David and Solomon had been divided and there was a King of only Judah. Not only that, there must have been "kings" of Judah.

It seems like the book was written before the captivity of Babylon, but well after the kingdom was split into the northern and southern kingdoms of Israel and Judah. There are also several countings of people in the book where Israel and Judah are listed as two factions of the country. The people would not have been counted this way until after the kingdom had divided.

1 Samuel Chapter 1

Elkanah And Hannah
1:1-8

It can often be confusing when we are told who people are and where they are from in the Old Testament. For instance, here in 1 Samuel it sounds like Elkanah is from the tribe of Ephraim because it tells us he is from a town in Ephraim. He is called a Zuphite and an Ephraimite. Both of these titles are confusing to us today, but they would have made more sense to the readers of the period.

Elkanah is actually a Levite by ancestry, which we

are told in 1 Chronicles 6:25-28. What our author here means by calling him a Zuphite and an Ephraimite is that Elkanah and his family resided in the land of Ephraim and in the town of Ramathaim Zuphim, another name for what we will be told is Samuel's hometown of Ramah.

Calling Elkanah an Ephraimite meant that he was a Levite who had settled in the tribe of Ephraim. Because the Levites had no inheritance in Israel, most of them were disbursed among the tribes as they were commanded so that the tribe God had withheld for Himself would have provision. It would have been too much for all the Levites and priests to be in one place with no provision for most of Israel's history up to this point. They were a reminder of God's provision to the Israelites.

> *That is why the Levites have no share or inheritance among their fellow Israelites; the LORD is their inheritance, as the LORD your God told them*
>
> *Deuteronomy 10:9*

For whatever reason, it does not seem like Elkanah had any priestly or levitical duty at the tabernacle in Shiloh, but he faithfully made the pilgrimage to Shiloh, where the tabernacle of Moses was at the time, to offer sacrifices.

Our author briefly mentions Hophni, Phinehas and Eli. One of the main things we will see in 1 Samuel is the transition away from the judges that led Israel to a monarchy. Eli happens to be one of the last judges over Israel and we will shortly be introduced to the last. We will return to them shortly and find out how things in Israel are going.

Elkanah, unfortunately, followed a common custom of the day to marry multiple wives. the Old Testament never honors or condemns the practice of polygamy, but we see in every instance that it is a horrible institution. It created unspeakable problems for both the women and men who decided to partake in it.

Poor Peninnah had married Elkanah and had born many sons and daughters, one of the highest honors of womanhood during that day, but unfortunately she was unloved. Elkanah had a favorite wife, and she was not it. Hannah, even though she had born Elkanah no children, was the wife he loved.

We see that it was the Lord who had closed Hannah's womb. One of the most difficult things to understand in life is how the Lord's plans for our lives intersect with His timing. Because of her situation and the redemptive plan over her life, Hannah was forced to suffer the scorn of her rival wife.

Why God allows us to suffer is often one of the hardest questions to wrestle with. Often, we get no answer from God for weeks, months, years and decades. It is only with great hindsight that we see and understand what He was doing. In the meantime, we often create more problems for ourselves when we grow restless with God's silence.

Instead of accepting her husband's doting love, Hannah could only see the things she did not have.

She wanted a son, and nothing less would ease her pain. It may have been her barrenness that caused Elkanah to marry again in the first place. Just like Abraham and Jacob, Elkanah may have been prodded along by a desperate woman to marry again to have children, a decision with regrettable consequences.

It was the common practice that when sacrifices were made at the tabernacle, some of the meat, flour and spices went to the priest, but the family that was offering the sacrifice would eat what was left. It was a holy meal, consumed as a reminder of God's never ending love and forgiveness of sins. It was this meal where our story of woe and regret begins to change for Hannah.

Hannah and Eli
1:9-20

At the annual sacrifice, Elkanah would give Hannah a double portion, which caused Peninnah great jealousy. It was at these occasions she would cause great trouble and pain for Hannah. It was under these circumstances that Hannah decided she'd had enough. Immediately after their meal, where she was forced to look across the table at a rival wife's mocking eyes, Hannah shot up and left.

In desperation, Hannah began to pray to the Lord before the tabernacle. She must not have realized that her lips were moving as she was silently praying. Her desperation was so great that she began to bargain with the Lord. How often when we are desperate do we initiate the same reasoning!

But God cannot be bargained with. We have nothing He needs. We have nothing to offer. It is only by His goodness that He considers the prayers offered through bargaining. Hannah's prayer was answered, not because she offered the Lord something He needed, but because she happened upon the divine timing of the Lord.

God was raising up an intercessor for Israel in the pattern of the One True intercessor to come. It was through Hannah's womb we would see one of the greatest examples of humility, leadership and concern for His people God would raise up until His only Son would come.

Eli saw Hannah praying in her desperation, and figured she must have gotten drunk from their sacrificial feast. Lips silently moving during a prayer must have been such an unusual sight in those days that Eli could think of no other cause for it.

Hannah quickly corrects Eli and tells him of her unspoken situation. In an attempt to bless her, we see the delegated authority Eli possesses by simply joining in her intercession, even though he is not an especially "holy" man. He asked that the Lord would grant her request, whatever it was.

Hannah's silent promise to the Lord may have been rash, but it was exactly what the Lord was looking for. Hannah may have been bargaining with the Lord, but what she was offering was actually the plan of the Lord all along. God had kept her from offering it until the time and situation with Eli and his family had reached a critical impasse.

We see that it was Eli's partnering prayer that would lead to the Lord opening Hannah's womb. She named her firstborn son Samuel, a word in Hebrew that means "heard by God."

SAMUEL
1:21-28

Hannah made a promise to the Lord to present the son she bargained for before Eli to be raised in the presence of the priests and the ark of the covenant, the earthy representation of the presence of God. She intended to make good on her promise, but like any loving mother, she chose to soak up every last moment she had with the young boy.

The oaths and bargains the people of the Old Testament made were often rash and regrettable, which is why Jesus would later tell us to simply let our "yes" be "yes" (Matthew 5:37). Even though swearing and oaths were often "from the evil one," God would use such oaths for His purposes. Elkanah knew he did not want to get in the way of Hannah offering her firstborn son to the Lord to be continually in His service.

When Samuel was old enough to be weaned, possibly about three years old, she took him to Eli at the time of their annual sacrifice. It must have been an odd moment for Eli, who was used to receiving the sacrifices from families across Israel, to receive a child.

It does not seem like this was a normal custom for people to engage in, and Hannah did not give Eli any opportunity to refuse her.

He was going to become the surrogate father and caretaker of Samuel whether he wanted to or not.

1 Samuel Chapter 2

Hannah's Song
2:1-11

Hannah's song is a prayer that expresses the raw emotions of her heart from years of having to share a husband with a bitter and scorned woman. All too often, we restrain from telling God exactly how we feel about things for fear of offending Him. We try and withhold our anger, envy, hatred, bitterness and jealousy thinking He does not want or need to know about those things. Nothing could be further from the truth.

Hannah holds nothing back. When we express the fullness of our emotions to God, He is able to help us wrestle with them and deal with them appropriately. How often do people bottle up their emotions only to take them out on the wrong people in inappropriate ways at inopportune times? How much better it would be if we laid everything we struggle with at God's feet as Hannah does here.

In her song, we see the depths of her despair from the scorn she received from Peninnah. We are given a hint from Hannah that this was possibly written after she had several more children by her acknowledgement that she had born "seven children." This could mean that Hannah's song is the teaching of a lifelong struggle with the Lord and Peninnah, or a prophetic assumption of what is to come.

One interesting thing that Hannah ends on is the acknowledgment of God giving strength to "His king." Is it possible that Samuel was not the first prophet in his family line?

HOPHNI AND PHINEHAS
2:12-26

One interesting point about Hannah leaving Samuel with Eli is that Eli was no longer priest of the Lord. He had taken something a retirement and appointed two of his sons, Hophni and Phinehas as priests in his place. If Hannah wanted Samuel to be continually before the presence of the Lord, why didn't she leave Samuel with the Lord's two current high priests?

She left Samuel with Eli instead of Hophni and Phinehas for good reason. Our author goes on now to tell us just how wicked the two sons of Eli were. Not only were they wicked men, they made no attempt to hide it from anyone. They helped themselves to what belonged to others, to the Lord and engaged in whatever illicit pleasure their hearts desired.

The biggest problem the Lord had with Hophni and Phinehas was not with their carousing or their thefts.

It was the fact that they treated the peoples' offerings before the Lord with contempt. Here were the two men who were supposed to be representing the Lord before the people and instructing them in His ways, actually turning people away from following God!

Eli confronted them about this very fact and pointed out a tragic truth to them. "Who will intercede for you if you sin against the Lord?" (2:25) How terrible a situation to be in for them!

Unfortunately for Eli and for all Israel, he chose to do nothing about them. It may have been that Eli was too old and his sons too abusive for him to remove them by force. It could have been that Eli was too bound by devotion to his sons to discipline them. Or, it may just have been that Eli was too complacent and complicit with what they were doing to stop them. We will see later that Eli had himself grown fat, literally on the gifts of the people of Israel.

Whatever Eli's reasons, the Lord had an opinion about it and He was sure to share it with him.

THE NAMELESS PROPHET
2:27-36

The prophet that the Lord sent to Eli had no name, home or origin. He appears much like Melchizedek does for Abraham. He is a reminder that no matter how bad things are, the Lord will always maintain control over His people, plans and purposes. He will always have someone whose heart turned to Him.

At this time in Israel, there was no one standing up for the things of the Lord. The witness of the God who created Adam, rescued Noah from destruction, covenanted with Abraham and rescued the Israelites from the Egyptians had gone completely silent. As Jesus once said, if the people did not cry out to testify of Him, the rocks would be commanded to do it (Luke 19:40). So is the case now. Because Eli had allowed his sons to show contempt for the Lord and His sacrifices before the people, God sent an unknown man that He had preserved from Hophni and Phinehas' corruption.

There is no other prophecy like this one found in scripture, so negative in every aspect. The depth of anger the Lord reveals to Eli is unprecedented. The finality of God's word to Eli shows us just how serious God was about the ongoing sin of the house of Eli and how seriously the Lord took it.

The nameless prophet's words will surely come to pass before we complete the books of Samuel. Their fulfillment will be a sign to Israel that God sees all, knows all and will lead His people even when they forsake Him entirely.

If only Eli had repented! If only his heart had been made contrite, would he have witnessed a different outcome? If God would reconsider the negatives He planned for wicked men like King Manasseh and King Ahab, would He have changed course for Eli if only he had turned his heart to the Lord?

We are not told what, if any at all, Eli's response was

to the nameless prophet, but we will soon see his response when he is confronted a second time with the sin of his household.

1 Samuel Chapter 3

The Call of Samuel
3:1-9

Many scholars believe that Samuel was around three years old when Hannah left him with Eli. By chapter three, it appears some time has passed. We were told in chapter two that Samuel was a boy wearing a linen ephod, a priestly garment. From a young age, Samuel had been employed in the constant activity of handling the sacrifices offered by visiting Israelites.

Samuel was constantly in the service of the Lord for eight to ten years by the time we see the story of chapter three. During that time Eli neglected one important aspect of Samuel's duty that speaks volumes of why his sons and Israel were in the situation they found themselves in.

Our author here tells us that Samuel "did not yet know the Lord." It is no surprise that the word of the Lord was rare in those days if Eli could not introduce even young Samuel to the Lord. How tragic to serve for years before the Lord but never to meet Him! Samuel ministered and slept before the ark of the covenant, that earthly representation of the presence of God, for years and never so much as encountered

Him one time.

There is a big difference between knowing about God and knowing Him. How many pastors, ministers, Sunday school teachers and leaders in church have gone years in the service of the Lord only to later discover that they never knew Him? Even John Wesley expressed his regret that he spent two years in America to "convert the Indians,"[1] but then discovered that he himself needed converting because he became convinced that he did not know the Lord either.

Our relationship to God is not built on service. It is not built on knowledge of scripture. We cannot help ourselves to heaven by being close to those who serve the Lord. There is only one way to commune with the God of creation, and that is to know Him personally. We must have our own ongoing, growing encounter with Him. At this point, Samuel did not have that, and neither did God's priests, Eli, Hophni or Phinehas.

God called Samuel's name several times, but he mistook the voice for Eli's. Samuel gave Eli a restless night until he realized it was God Himself calling out to Samuel. He told Samuel exactly what to do from that point on and it would lead to Samuel actually knowing the Lord instead of just serving Him.

SAMUEL'S PROPHECY
3:10-21

It seems like Eli knew the word Samuel received from the Lord would be about him. We do not know if the Lord only addressed Eli twice about he and his sons, but Eli seems to have had that initial word on the forefront of his thoughts.

What an amazing thing it is to hear from the Lord, but it must have been a terrifying encounter for young Samuel to hear what the Lord had to say about Eli, the man who had been his caretaker for years now. Samuel probably knew just how wicked Hophni and Phinehas were, but Eli never turned Samuel over into their care; he stayed with Eli the entire time. At least Eli had done that for Hannah's sake, or maybe at her specific direction. Samuel must have hurt for Eli to receive such a message about the man who raised him.

What is interesting about Eli's inquisition of Samuel is not that he threatened Samuel to tell him everything, but that he just accepted the word as it was. Again, what if Eli had repented? What if he had asked the Lord for mercy?

We will never know what could have been, because Eli was resigned to accept whatever fate was to befall he and his lineage. How sad.

As for Samuel, this was the first of a long life of the Lord speaking to him on a very intimate basis. The Lord spoke often and powerfully to Samuel so that in a very short period of time everyone in Israel had heard of him and his reputation as a seer (later called a prophet) was solidified.

[1]http://wesley.nnu.edu/john-wesley/john-wesley-the-methodist/chapter-vi-to-america-and-back/

Don't forget to read 1 Samuel this week!
Visit 10WeekBible.com for more resources including daily podcasts, videos and more.

1 Samuel 4-6

Study Questions

1. Why did Samuel become so famous in Israel?

2. Why did the Israelites take the ark of the covenant into battle against the Philistines?

3. What piece of news did Eli receive that actually caused him to die? What is significant about that?

WEEK 2 | 1 SAMUEL 4-6

4. What happened to the Philistines while they had the ark of the covenant?

5. Does God hear the cries of pagan people who do not know or worship Him? Does He hear the cries of people today who do not serve Him?

6. What was significant and supernatural about the plan the Philistines came up with to return the ark?

7. Why did God kill the people of Beth Shemesh for peeking inside the ark? What was the harm in a little peek?

8. Did God judge the Israelites by a different standard than the Philistines? Does He judge people differently today?

COMMENTARY NOTES

1 SAMUEL CHAPTER 4

Samuel became famous in Israel. This is a very important detail about Samuel. It sets him apart from all the other judges in Israel's history. Most of the other judges became famous when the Lord raised them up to deliver His people, but Samuel's fame was established long before he ever led a military campaign.

What is most important is not that he became famous, but why he became so well known.

THE PROPHETIC MINISTRY RESTORED
4:1

Many people have been taught that prophecy is what happens in the Bible when a prophetic writer pens an eternal revelation of God's glory that is captured in the Canon of Scripture. While this is definitely prophetic, it is far from the normal operation of prophetic ministry.

Normal prophetic ministry is deeply personal and seldom has anything to do with the redemptive purposes of Israel as revealed in scripture. When the Bible tells us that Samuel's words came to all Israel, what it means is that when the people of Israel would visit the tabernacle to offer sacrifices, Samuel would regularly prophesy over them in a deeply personal way.

It is incredibly powerful to know that God sees you and hears you. Samuel made all Israel understand that God saw and heard them. Most people struggle through life wondering if God actually knows them, if He cares about them or if anything they do matters to Him. When there is little revelation, as was the case as we started this book, people wander away from the Lord. It is harder to keep our focus on the Lord when we are not sure if He actually cares about the things we do.

But now the nation has Samuel. Samuel was prophesying over individuals and for the first time in their lives this God whom they sacrificed to was not so far off, but deeply interested in them and very personal.

Subjective, contemporary prophecy, as opposed to objective, eternal scriptural prophecy, is exactly what Paul claimed was the most important of all spiritual gifts God gives in 1 Corinthians 14. It is because when we actually know God, like Samuel did, instead of just knowing about Him, are our lives transformed.

> *Follow the way of love and eagerly desire gifts of the Spirit, especially prophecy. For anyone who speaks in a tongue does not speak to people but to God. Indeed, no one understands them; they utter mysteries by the Spirit. But the one who prophesies speaks to people for their strengthening, encouraging and comfort. Anyone who speaks in a tongue edifies themselves, but the one who prophesies edifies the church.*
>
> *1 Corinthians 14:1-4*

Samuel's fame did not come because he was a great teacher, but because he asked the Lord to speak to him about the people who stood before him when they came to offer sacrifices. That same prophetic spirit that Paul commanded us to eagerly seek above all other gifts was available to Samuel then is available to us today.

RAIDERS OF THE ARK
4:2-11

It doesn't take long for our author to introduce us to the arch rival of Israel. The Philistines bordered Israel to the southwest and lived along the Mediterranean. They grew wealthy over time through sea trade and were able to purchase armaments from the Egyptians. In vast quantities. As with most of the surrounding nations, they worshipped pagan idols and were hungry for more land. They regularly challenged the border lines of Israel.

The Philistines moved north and camped at Aphek so the Israelites camped opposite them in Ebenezer. The battle took place between the two villages and the Philistines won the initial campaign, causing the Israelites to retreat back to their stronghold.

The Israelites were so sure that they should have won, they were incredulous at the loss. Instead of inquiring of the Lord, they assumed that if they had the ark of the covenant with them in battle, like their ancestors had when they traveled through the wilderness, God would give them victories like He did for

WEEK 2 | 1 SAMUEL 4-6

Moses and Joshua.

Our author points out that the Lord sits enthroned between the cherubim atop the ark. The ark was not the actual home of the Lord, but a figurative representation of His glory. No image was ever to be made of Israel's God Most High, but the cherubs were the images of those beings that sit in closest fellowship with the Father.

When Joshua carried the ark with him through the battles to conquer the promised land, He regularly inquired of the Lord. When a battle was lost, the Lord told them why (Joshua 7). It was not the ark that was the Israelites' good-luck charm, but the Lord of all creation who ordered their steps.

When the Israelites sent for the ark in their current campaign, they treated it more like an idol that armies would have with them to incite their deities to cast fear into their enemies. When the Philistines heard about the ark, it did just that. They thought of it as a foreign god that they had heard stories about. Theirs was the "god" who defeated the mighty Egyptians. The Israelites "god" was the one who helped them successfully conquer the Canaanites. Now, it was this same "god" who stood before them and the greatest fear the Philistines had ever known gripped them.

In a scene out of a Hollywood epic, some mighty leader got up among the Philistines and told them if they did not reject their fear and fight like they had never fought before, they would be permanently subjected to the Israelites. As it was, the Philistines exercised a considerable amount of control over Israel. Later we will see that the Philistines had so much control that they would not allow blacksmiths the exist within Israel so they would be dependent on them for metal work, inhibiting them from creating their own weapons.

That day the Philistines fought, and they indeed won with an incredible victory. Thirty thousand men dying in that day was a very significant loss to Israel, not only in terms of the army, but in terms of economic production and population. The loss of human life was great, but worst of all was the loss of the ark of the covenant of God.

Losing the ark was far worse to the Israelites than any loss of human life. To many, it had become little more than an idol representing their god, but to many still is was the real earthly seat of the God Most High, their creator and defender. Losing it meant that the Lord must have left them, a pain far worse than the pain of the loss of their friends and family.

ELI, HOPHNI AND PHINEHAS DIE
4:12-22

When the young man from Benjamin told the news to the people of Shiloh, it is interesting that he didn't stop first to tell Eli what had happened. Eli was sitting by the road, waiting for news to come. Eli was worried, and with good reason.

Eli was old, and he knew his days were numbered.

He had been told twice that the Lord was going to take his sons' lives on the same day, and this battle must have seemed like the time that would happen. Blind and fattened by years of taking the fatty, stolen meat his sons demanded from the children of Israel, the Benjamite passed right by him and told the townspeople of the despair that had befallen them.

It wasn't until Eli heard the cries from within the town that he suspected his worst fears had come to pass. If you have ever heard the wails of mothers who have been told that their children are now dead, then you can understand why Eli was concerned, but Eli's greatest fear wasn't for his sons.

Eli must have already made some sort of peace that the sins of his sons would be their undoing, the Lord had promised him as much. Something else had troubled Eli. It was that on this day when he suspected his sons would die, they chose to take the ark of the covenant into battle with them. In fact, Hophni and Phinehas were the ark's caretakers, so Eli had great cause for concern for the welfare of the ark.

Eli caught the attention of the messenger and inquired what was going on. It was when the Benjamite mentioned the ark, not his sons, that Eli fell backward. His age combined with his weight snapped his neck and he died there. The last words Eli heard were that the ark had been captured.

Not surprisingly, Phinehas' wife was also troubled. She gave birth to a son on this most terrible of days. What is also not surprising, is that even she was not so broken up about her husband's passing as she was about the loss of the ark. Phinehas was not the most faithful of husbands. Our author has already told us that he and his brother had a habit of sleeping with the prostitutes they allowed to camp out at the entrance to the tabernacle.

With her last breath, Phinehas' wife gives her orphan son the prophetic name Ichabod, "The glory has departed."

This was a tragic moment in the life of Israel, but one that the Lord was going to use to show His people that He and the ark were not one. God had not departed from Israel. Far from it. In fact, God was going to use this period of time to show just how great His name was without any need of His chosen people to help Him out.

1 Samuel Chapter 5

The ark had been lost and for a brief moment, it appears that all hope was lost. But God was not done. With the death of Eli, one of the last judges of the Lord, God had something truly great in store for Israel.

In Philistine Territory
5:1-12

One of the last and strongest people groups within the land of Canaan since the Israelites began to occu-

WEEK 2 | 1 SAMUEL 4-6

py it was the Philistines. With the loss to them in the previous chapter's campaign, we see that they are incredibly strong indeed. This may very well have been the height of their civilization. The Lord was prepared to deal with them now as He had the other wicked peoples of the land of Canaan whom the Israelites had displaced.

Many historians believe that Samson's reign as judge and the death of Eli are closely related to one another. It does seem that there was overlap, but exactly how that looked, no is sure about. It is at least interesting to think about the fact that at the time the Philistines had captured the ark and routed Israel that God would have raised up two of the greatest deliverers of Israel from Philistia almost simultaneously, Samson and Samuel.

As we read this chapter, it also begs the question; how did the Israelites know so much about what was going on in Philistia during the time the ark was there? Could it possibly have been Samson who relayed all this information to his fellow countrymen?

One of the greatest stories of God mocking idols in scripture is that He caused Dagon to fall and bow before the ark of the covenant two days in a row. The Philistines chalked the first collapse of their deaf and dumb carving to chance. The second night was unmistakable. Combined with the new tumors that were appearing all over the people and the fact that when they opened the doors to the temple of Dagon in the morning and found his head and hands there, they knew the "gods" of the Israelites were against them.

The supernatural destruction of the idol of Dagon was so alarming to the Philistines, the priests henceforth refused to step on the threshold of the temple since they found the broken head and hands of their demonic god's idol laying there.

From Ashdod they moved the ark to Gath and from Gath to Ekron. Everywhere the ark went, the Lord caused sickness, panic and death to overtake that city. There were tumors afflicting the people as well as an infestation of rats that more than likely carried the diseases.

There was so much death and panic that by the time the Philistines moved the ark to Ekron, the people saw it coming and cried out for them to keep it away. They feared the same death and pestilence would come to them.

We end this chapter with a most interesting phrase, "the outcry of the city went up to heaven."

This is a similar phrase used throughout scripture that when the Israelites would become oppressed by foreign nations, they would cry out to God and their cries would be heard. Here we see a very clear place in the Old Testament where we are told that God heard the cries of a pagan people. They were crying out to Him, even if they were not fully aware of it, to heal them and free them from the death and pain that had overtaken them.

God's Word is full of God's love for people, even people who oppose Him most of the time. We all were once rebellious people who God showed His love for by dying for us while we were yet in sin.

1 Samuel Chapter 6

How did God answer the Philistines' cries? By giving a clear plan to the worst of the Philistines: the priests and diviners of their false gods.

The Plan
6:1-9

For seven months the ark was in Philistine territory. For seven long months, their people were tormented by painful tumors and death. Fear gripped them because the Lord was making a clear distinction between the One True God of Israel and the false gods of nations like Philistia. This was actually a moment of grace to the Philistines unlike any other in scripture.

With no ties to winning wars with other nations' gods, the Philistines were coming into contact with the only God on their own turf, apart from any Israeli interaction. This was their opportunity to turn their hearts to Him, but unfortunately, national pride still remained greater than their desire for truth and life.

Still, the Lord was kind to them and gave them a way to overcome what had befallen them for the theft of the ark. God gave them a supernatural plan.

Their priests and diviners formed a plan to send the ark back to Israel that could only work with the help of the divine. They chose a plan that went contrary to the nature of the created order, and by doing so they assured themselves that it truly was God they were encountering and not just random bad luck.

They took two cows who had young calves that would have wanted to suckle and penned up their calves. They yoked the cows to the cart they built to carry the ark. These cows had never been yoked before, something that took a lot of training for cows to respond favorably to. They placed offerings of gold into a box on the cart in the form of their pestilence; the tumors and rats.

If the cows went straight into Israeli territory instead of turning back to find their calves, then it would mean that it was definitely the God of Israel that had struck them. The natural inclination of the mother cows was to find their calves and nurse them. If they refused this and instead went to Israel, without being led to do so, the Philistines knew that Israel's God would forgive them their trespass of stealing the ark.

God did not need Israel to be militarily victorious to distinguish Himself as the God of Israel. He is very skilled at showing that Himself. He showed the Philistines that there is One True God, the Creator of heaven and earth, and He is the unseen God of the Israelites of whom no image was ever to be made.

The Plan Fulfilled
6:10-18

The plan worked like a charm. It did not work because it was easy for the cows to do what they did, but it worked because there was a very real God causing them to do what was unnatural. The cows, who had never walked along a road with a yoke before did not deviate from it until they reached Israelites. A cow's natural habitat is a pasture, not a road.

The Philistine plan was not just to send back the ark to Israel, but was a kind of "Gideon's fleece" to see whether the devastation had been brought about by Israel's God. Imagine how amazed they must have been when everything they were testing came to pass!

The aristocrats of the Philistines followed the ark at a distance to see what would happen. Imagine being the people of Beth Shemesh in their fields as they saw the ark coming and the Philistines behind it. Their first impulse was joy, but there must have been a little fear next as they realized their mortal enemies were right behind it. Without a word being spoken, the Philistine rulers watched as the people of Beth Shemesh cut up the cart, butchered the cows and sacrificed them before the Lord. One can imagine a nod between the mayor of Beth Shemesh and the king of Ekron standing off in the distance before they departed.

It was certainly a day filled with joy for the people of Beth Shemesh as they realized the Lord had honored them with the return of their sacred treasure back to

Israel. Unfortunately, their joy would be short-lived.

PEEKING INSIDE
6:19-7:2

The Lord used the ark's time in Philistine territory to convince them that He was a holy God. He was not like the false deities they and the other pagan nations around them worshipped. They remembered the stories of what happened to the Egyptians generations ago and now they were experiencing the heavy hand of a holy God themselves. They had known better than to harden their hearts against Him, which is why they sent the ark back to Beth Shemesh in the first place.

If only the people of Israel had held the ark in such reverence. When God told Moses to create the ark, it was to hold a few important remnants of their time in Israel, but then be shut up and never viewed again. It was similar in design to the tree of the knowledge of good and evil. The Lord placed a test there for the people to know what it was, but that they weren't to touch it.

The temptation was too much for the people of Beth Shemesh. They had heard that it was filled with the articles of their exodus, but they had never seen them before. The Lord had promised them if they touched it, they would die. There must have been a similar temptation from the enemy as in the early days of humanity where they were convinced that "surely they would not die."

Because they did what the Lord had very seriously told them not to do, He caused many of the people of Beth Shemesh to die for peeking inside. God does not show favoritism, and He was not going to treat the Israelites any more leniently than the Philistines for treating Him with less than the honor and obedience He deserved.

The people of Beth Shemesh then became afraid of the Lord and the ark and they sent it to the priests of Kiriath Jearim, where it would stay for the next twenty years.

The Rumors Of Our Deaths Are Greatly Exaggerated
6:19

1 Samuel 6:19 contains one of the more famous (and rare) copyist errors in scripture. Some of the most ancient manuscripts of scripture here say that it was 50,700 people who the Lord put to death. The obvious problem with this is that there were not, to anyone's knowledge, any cities in Israel of this size. Beth Shemesh certainly was not this big.

The fact that this discrepancy exists calls many people to question the authority of scripture. This is indeed a noted copyist error, but one thing is certain about every copyist error in Scripture. Because the scribes who copied the Bible by hand took their job so seriously, when an error from ancient times was in the manuscript, they still copied it anyway.

Josh McDowel's book, <u>Evidence That Demands a Verdict</u> is a good read for anyone interested in how accurate the Bible is. Based on the number of errors, the amount of copies of scripture in existence and the length of time it has been copied by hand, there is no other document in history that comes anywhere close to the accuracy of the Bible, Old and New Testament. No other document in history has been handled with the care and holiness than the Bible.

Don't forget to read 1 Samuel this week!
Visit 10WeekBible.com for more resources including daily podcasts, videos and more.

1 Samuel 7-9

Study Questions

1. Why did the Israelites need to repent? Do we still need to repent today?

2. Why were the Philistines attacking Israel again?

3. Why did Samuel instruct the army to fast just before an attack? Was this wise? Should we still fast today, and what for?

4. What did it mean to be a judge in Israel in Samuel's day? What would we call Samuel today in his capacity to lead Israel?

5. Did the Israelites really reject Samuel because of his sons? If not, why did Israel reject Samuel?

6. What does it mean to reject the Lord?

7. What was causing the Israelites to ask for a king?

8. Why didn't the Israelites just ask for Samuel to mount a counterattack against Nahash?

COMMENTARY NOTES

1 SAMUEL CHAPTER 7

REPENTANCE
7:2-6

During the time of the Judges of Israel, God's chosen people followed a very routine and sadly predictable pattern. They would forget about the Creator God who saved and delivered them and turn away after other gods of the nations that surrounded them. This was a way to indulge themselves in all the debauchery of pagan nations and throw off the shackles of their very moral God.

After a while living in sin, the Lord would send foreign oppressors, an obvious nod at the uselessness of their idols in the first place, to conquer His people. The people would fight their oppressors at first, eventually give up and accept their cruel rule.

During that period of occupation, the Israelites would begin to remember the God who had delivered their people from the hands of the Egyptians. They would remind each other of the previous times when God would send a judge to lead them and free them from their unwelcome masters. That salvation would always and only come on the heels of one thing: repentance.

The Lord would always stall His deliverance until

the cries of His people reached a threshold. We are not told what number that was, but it was always deeply rooted in repentance.

Here in 1 Samuel 7 we see that heart of repentance. It was because the people of Israel had come face to face with a very real and a very holy God. It is not unlike a story that Luke tells us in Acts 19.

> *Some Jews who went around driving out evil spirits tried to invoke the name of the Lord Jesus over those who were demon-possessed. They would say, "In the name of the Jesus whom Paul preaches, I command you to come out." Seven sons of Sceva, a Jewish chief priest, were doing this. One day the evil spirit answered them, "Jesus I know, and Paul I know about, but who are you?" Then the man who had the evil spirit jumped on them and overpowered them all. He gave them such a beating that they ran out of the house naked and bleeding.*
>
> *When this became known to the Jews and Greeks living in Ephesus, they were all seized with fear, and the name of the Lord Jesus was held in high honor. Many of those who believed now came and openly confessed what they had done. A number who had practiced sorcery brought their scrolls together and burned them publicly. When they calculated the value of the scrolls, the total came to fifty thousand drachmas. In this way the word of the Lord spread widely and grew in power.*
>
> *Acts 19:13-20*

Much like the awakening that happened in Acts 19, the death-toll related to the people of Beth Shemesh looking inside the Ark struck fear into the hearts of the Israelites. Here they were, worshipping at the feet of carved and cast idols that they had made themselves. They were worshipping idols that could not speak and could not deliver, but they had just encountered a God what was real, alive and powerful.

It was the death of those who looked inside the ark that caused all Israel to repent before the Lord, the One True God of all the earth. They did not want to hold onto anything else anymore, and it was because of this that God raised up a new judge to deliver them from the Philistines.

Samuel already sat over Israel as a judge, to some extent, since he prophesied so frequently and accurately over them as they came to Moses' tent. Now God was going to use him to deliver His people as all the other judges had.

Samuel called together the people of Israel at Mizpah, not necessarily for battle, but to repent. When they assembled, the entire nation fasted that day and confessed their sin before the Lord. They put away all their foreign idols and with one heart returned to the Lord. This is the kind of thing that can only happen when the Lord stirs hearts.

THE ASSEMBLY
7:7-9

When Samuel called all the people to assemble at Mizpah, it drew the ire of the Philistines. They saw this as a brazen act of war, assembling so close to their currently-occupied borders. It is interesting that this was not just a response by the Philistines that they were so quickly able to respond to the gathering of Israelites. In those days, even a standing army would have taken time to move opposite of Mizpah, so to be on the ready the day of their fasting is no coincidence.

The Israelites were again under the oppression of Philistia and they had cried out to the Lord in repentance to save them from a very real and a very current threat. The Philistines were obviously assembled for another assault on Israel to capture more territory. When you look at possible timelines of Israel's history during the times of the judges, most scholars believe that Eli, Samuel and Samson lived concurrently. Was this new raid by the Philistines in response to Samson's dying blow to the Philistine aristocracy found in Judges 16?

> *Now the rulers of the Philistines assembled to offer a great sacrifice to Dagon their god and to celebrate, saying, "Our god has delivered Samson, our enemy, into our hands."*
>
> *When the people saw him, they praised their god, saying,*
>
> *"Our god has delivered our enemy*

into our hands,

the one who laid waste our land

and multiplied our slain."

While they were in high spirits, they shouted, "Bring out Samson to entertain us." So they called Samson out of the prison, and he performed for them.

When they stood him among the pillars, Samson said to the servant who held his hand, "Put me where I can feel the pillars that support the temple, so that I may lean against them." Now the temple was crowded with men and women; all the rulers of the Philistines were there, and on the roof were about three thousand men and women watching Samson perform. Then Samson prayed to the Lord, "Sovereign Lord, remember me. Please, God, strengthen me just once more, and let me with one blow get revenge on the Philistines for my two eyes." Then Samson reached toward the two central pillars on which the temple stood. Bracing himself against them, his right hand on the one and his left hand on the other, Samson said, "Let me die with the Philistines!" Then he pushed with all his might, and down came the temple on the rulers and all the people in it. Thus he killed many more when he died than while he lived.

Judges 16:23-30

This seems to have happened after the ark had spent time in the temple of Dagon, so this quite possibly could have been the reason for the current Philistine angst agains Israel.

Fasting For Victory
7:10-14

Samuel's assembly was most definitely military in nature, but his choice of attack was most unusual.

When planning an assault against a very powerful and well-equipped military state, fasting is not a good idea. More than just making you hungry, fasting makes you weak, something that is not at all helpful when preparing to engage in hand-to-hand combat. Yet this is the strategy that the Lord gave to Samuel. The Lord wanted to show His chosen people that it was not their might, their weaponry or their skill that had ever saved them. It was Him and Him alone.

While Samuel was offering a sacrifice of grilled meat in the midst of an army of men weak from fasting, the Philistines ran forward to attack. It was then that the Lord sent His mighty thunder to terrify the Philistines. It is unlikely that the thunder came from a rain storm. Armies would rarely engage in open battle in inclement weather because it could take away any advantage they had.

This thunder was most likely not from a storm, but a localized thunder among the Philistines on a clear day. It sent shivers down their spine and they turned and ran, leaving their weapons, armor and belongings behind as the Israelites pursued.

One of the most amazing things about this battle is

that it not only freed the Israelites, but the Amorites as well. Samuel's supernatural victory liberated more territory than anyone alive had seen up to that time.

ISRAEL'S LAST JUDGE
7:15-17

Samuel had already acted as a judge over Israel before this battle, but it was always a military victory that firmly established someone as a ruler over the people. This established Samuel as Israel's judge. Unfortunately, he would be their last for reasons we will deal with in the coming chapters.

Samuel was a circuit-riding judge. He would travel around a relatively small area and hold court to decide matters between the people. One other thing that Samuel did that is not expressly mentioned here is to establish schools of prophets. Undoubtedly, Samuel would make this circuit to hold court but also to give instruction and further grow the fledgling schools that would soon appear all over Israel.

In truth, Samuel's greatest legacy were these schools that receive no mention here. By the end of his life, Samuel's Israel was a much different place than when he was young and there "weren't many visions." We will see very shortly their scope and impact in Israel.

1 Samuel Chapter 8

Samuel's Sons
8:1-5

Between chapters seven and eight an entire generation passes and we are quickly faced with a sad new reality. Samuel has handed off control of the nation to his sons and entered a kind of retirement.

There is much that Samuel may have been able to learn from people like James Dobson about parenting, but in the end a person's path is his own and no parent can force their will or lifestyle on their children. For his sons, the power of ruling over Israel was too much for them to handle. Money, power and fame from a young age all too often have devastating consequences on those who have not faced the trials of life that allow them to cope with their position.

Imagine yourself in Samuel's shoes. When all the aristocrats of Israel appeared before him in his hometown and asked him to step down as leader of Israel so they could have a king, it must have been devastating. It hurt Samuel on many levels.

No More Repentance
8:6-10

On one level, Samuel was hurt because he was being asked to step down as their leader. This must have hurt personally in the worst way. On another level,

Samuel had been Israel's conscience and prophet for a generation when almost none had existed before him. He knew what they were asking for and how bad it would be for them.

Samuel immediately took the matter to the Lord, like he did all things. We have much to learn from the few short pages in scripture about Samuel. How often, when faced with such a moment as this, do we immediately turn to God for answers?

The Lord reassured Samuel that it was not actually him they were rejecting, but the Lord Himself. It is impossible to understand this rejection without knowledge of the pattern of the judges we have already spoken of. The cycle of deliverance by God, turning away from God, God raising up oppressors, crying out and repenting and deliverance by God was now well-known to the Israelites and they wanted something new.

The Israelites had no standing army. They had no defined leader, no electoral college, no dictator and no monarchy. This notion that the Lord would select whom He chose at a time of His choosing based on Israel's fidelity to Him seemed like nonsense all of a sudden. As the aristocrats of Israel looked around at other nations, they noticed something very different.

Other nations had kings who provided standing armies, weapons and protection that the Israelites did not have. In fact, when viewed in light of other nations, the way the Israelites were living looked like madness now. The leaders wanted protection and they wanted it in a new way. An easier way. They wanted it without having to look to the Lord for it.

That is where things had gone awry. Up to this point, the Lord had been Israel's leader. With no king and no military, they had done an amazing thing. They had unseated and conquered territory held by established monarchies with standing armies. Has there ever been a people like this before or since in human history? The Lord had always led them expertly and only demanded one thing in return: allegiance to Him alone.

This was the one thing the leaders were no longer willing to give the Lord. This new request for a king was really a refusal to repent. The people had again begun to worship idols so that they could engage in the kind of immoral lifestyle those deaf and dumb gods allowed. And now they were faced again with mounting threats that they could not handle alone.

Our author does not mention here the threat they were encountering, but at this very moment one of the most fearful oppressors of Israel was currently besieging Jabesh Gilead. We are told in 1 Samuel 11 that Nahash, king of the Ammonites had sent shockwaves of fear throughout Israel. But Nahash's conquest did not begin in chapter eleven. It had begun some time earlier and the siege of Jabesh Gilead took some time. It was because of this current threat that the people of Israel asked for a king.

A WICKED REQUEST
8:11-22

In light of the knowledge of the attack from Nahash, this request takes on new light. It was not because Israel just wanted a king or because they didn't like Samuel's sons that they wanted a king. It was because they needed someone to rescue them from their oppressors and they were tired of having to repent before God would help them.

The other nations around the Israelites all had kings and the people did not need to repent to the One True God for protection. Those nations had kings with standing armies, swords, spears, shields and every other piece of military hardware for ongoing protection. The Israelites were jealous of the nations who were subduing them because they did not have to submit their hearts to the Lord.

Samuel told the people all the things that their king would do *to* them, not *for* them. The people were only thinking of their continued safety, not the negatives of what they were asking for. Little did they know that their first king would not not only fail to supply for their safety, but he would lay ahold of his rights and then some as enumerated by Samuel here.

Up until this time, the people did not know taxes. That may seem trivial, but imagine how much different your life would be without taxes. Imagine how much more you could do without taxes. Imagine how much less stressful your life would be without them. That is what the Israelite's lives were like up until this point.

Samuel told them that their coming king would take from them the very best of what they had. Their offerings to the Lord were supposed to be the best of what they had with the promise from the Lord that He would repay many times over what they had sacrificed. With a king, there was no free will offering and there was no repayment. Cattle, donkeys, fields, labor, children and anything else the king wanted he would take.

Samuel prophesied to the Israelites on that day. We have no specific fulfillment of his prophecy written for us in scripture, but we can be sure from the events that would unfold that his prophecy surely came true. Samuel told the people that because they asked for a king for such a wicked reason, God was not going to listen to their prayers on the day when they asked Him to take away their king.

What a horrible prophecy! Samuel forewarned the people that no matter how desperately they asked, God was not going to remove their first king from them until His time was complete. The Israelites had no idea what an amazing thing they had going for them, and God was going to forever change it.

Samuel did not only proclaim all this to the Israelites, but he also took all his words, most probably written down in some form, and repeated them directly before the Lord. Samuel truly lived differently. He believed it was just as important to speak before the Lord the very same things he said publicly. The courts of heaven truly mattered just as much to Samuel as the testimony of man. If only the same could be said of us today!

The Lord's word at that point does not seem very clear. He told Samuel to give the people a king, almost like Samuel had the discretion to choose, but instead of choosing from among the elders who were standing before him them, he refrained and sent them all away. Samuel was one who followed the Lord with all his heart, but he also knew how to carry himself in front of people. He knew that if he appointed a leader from among the people and it seemed like his own choosing, that the people may reject it the same as him appointing his sons to lead in his place.

Samuel chose to send everyone home and wait for an opportune time to appoint a king. He was surely waiting on the Lord, but he was also waiting for an opportunity to make sure everyone know without a doubt that the choice of king was God's choice and not his own.

That time was soon to come.

1 Samuel Chapter 9

Before we continue on, it is important to understand just why the choice of a Benjamin is so peculiar for Israel's king. The Lord has a habit of choosing people from unexpected places, especially those who seem to be of lesser importance. The tribe of Benjamin was just such a tribe. The final three chapters of the book of Judges tells a tragic story of the decimation of the tribe of Benjamin. Once a powerful part of Israel, Benjamin was reduced to a small fraction of Israel's population.

Saul was from the smallest tribe in Israel, not because they had failed to grow and thrive, but because they were destroyed by their fellow Israelites for a wickedness that rivaled that of Sodom and Gomorrah.

The second reason the choice of Benjamin is interesting is because from as far back as Jacob himself, Judah had been proclaimed as the tribe to rule over the others. Messianic prophecies about Judah had been around as long as Judah had, so why did God choose Benjamin instead of Judah for Israel's first king?

We will soon read that God would "regret" making Saul king. We must not mistake God saying He regretted something for Him not knowing what was to come. Somehow in God's wisdom, He allows for people to follow their own path while still falling into His plan. God's regret would not be an admission of a mistake He made, but an expression of the emotions He would feel over His people Israel.

INTRODUCING SAUL
9:1-10

Saul was everything the people of Israel would have wanted in a king. He was massive. The Jews today are not known for being an overly large people, and we know from history that people have gradually grown taller over time. The fact that Saul was a head taller than a very homogenous group of small people would have been quite the sight.

Saul had already started his own family, but he was still living on his immediate family's land. When his father's donkeys went missing, he sent his grown son out to search for them. Land-working livestock in those days was wealth, so Kish was in essence sending Saul out to find the money that had wandered away from their farm.

Saul seemed to take this opportunity to have a sightseeing vacation for himself, rather than focusing on the donkey search. The distance he and his servant travel looks more like a joyride than a search and rescue mission.

After having wandered around for a while, Saul and his servant decided to get serious about finding the donkeys, probably not coincidentally when they ran out of food. They just happened to be near Ramah and the servant had heard that Samuel lived there. They decided to take what little money they had left to pay for a prophecy.

PROPHETIC DESTINY
9:11-27

Saul and his servant arrived in town just in time for a celebration. What they were not aware of was that the celebration was in their honor! The day before Saul arrived, the Lord had spoken clearly to Samuel all the details about Saul and that he was to be anointed king of Israel. As soon as Samuel saw Saul this day, the Lord spoke to him and told him this was the new king.

Saul must have been shocked when he asked a random person where to find Samuel only to find he was speaking to him. Samuel told Saul about the donkeys and then he alluded to something far grander than Saul had on his mind that day.

We must understand that when the elders of Israel asked Samuel for a king, Samuel told them God was going to give them a king and to go home and wait for it. You know how the rumor mill works. By this time, certainly everyone in Israel was watching and waiting for Samuel to anoint the new ruler. Saul seems to immediately understand what Samuel is talking about when he says that all Israel's desire it turned toward him.

Saul rebuffs Samuel's statement by clarifying that he is from a small tribe and a small clan. Due to the tribal nature of Israel, the people felt like it was the larger tribes who carried the greatest strength. Most people probably assumed that it would be Manasseh or Judah or some other large tribe that their king would come from. God had something different planned for them.

Saul ate with Samuel that day and was given the place of honor and a cut of meat that Samuel set aside specifically for him. That night, Saul stayed with

Samuel and they spent the evening talking. Oh, to be a fly on the wall for that conversation!

The next morning, Samuel sent the servant away but kept Saul around. Samuel did not want anyone around to see what he was about to do, but why? Why didn't Samuel want anyone but Saul to know that he had been anointed king? We will have to read on to find out.

Don't forget to read 1 Samuel this week!
Visit 10WeekBible.com for more resources including daily podcasts, videos and more.

4

1 Samuel 10-12

Study Questions

1. Why did Samuel make sure that his anointing of Saul and prophetic words were given in private?

2. Why did people ask if Saul was among the prophets? What did they mean by that?

3. After anointing Saul king privately, why did Samuel use the Urim and Thummim to single out Saul for kingship in front of Israel?

4. Who was Nahash and why was he a problem?

5. How did Saul call all Israel together for battle against the Ammonites? What was his method reminiscent of?

6. Why was it so bad for Israel to ask for a king? What were they trying to bypass?

7. Have there been times in your life when you tried to bypass the way the Lord wanted to lead your life? When was a time chose a king over giving your life entirely over to the Lord's leadership?

Commentary Notes

1 Samuel Chapter 10

Prophetic Anointing
10:1-8

Samuel did not want anyone but Saul to be around for his anointing. For a man who had done so many things very publicly, why did Samuel choose to anoint Saul in private? There are probably several reasons, but one that is very clear is that he did not want anyone but Saul to hear the prophetic word he was about to decree over Saul.

This prophetic word is what Saul would later be judged by in his actions as king. Nowhere in scripture will you find such a set of specific instructions to follow. God was so clear here with Saul that this should be perceived as a test. When the Lord spoke to Moses, Aaron and Miriam about the rebellion against Moses, He said this:

> *"When there is a prophet among you,*
> *I, the Lord, reveal myself to them in visions,*
> *I speak to them in dreams.*
> *But this is not true of my servant Moses;*
> *he is faithful in all my house.*
> *With him I speak face to face,*
> *clearly and not in riddles;*

> *he sees the form of the Lord.*
> *Why then were you not afraid*
> *to speak against my servant Moses?"*
>
> *Numbers 12:6-8*

The clear indication is that for most prophetic people, riddles, dreams and mysteries is how God normally speaks. If the Lord does speak so clearly, as He did to Moses, it is clear that a high degree of obedience is required. The Lord almost put Moses to death for failing to circumcise his own children (Exodus 4:24-26) after his encounter at the burning bush!

Sometimes the Lords speaks clearly about things that are shortly to take place and seemingly inconsequential to give us faith for the real message that is yet to come. That is exactly what happened here with Saul. Two men telling him about the donkeys, three men offering bread and a company of prophets he would join in with: these three things seem trivial for the newly anointed king, but they were the Lord showing Saul that this word was definitely from Him, and obedience to the most crucial part would be critical.

It is the message about Gilgal that was the important part of Samuel's prophecy. This meeting where Saul was to wait seven days for Samuel to offer a sacrifice was still months away, possibly even more than a year away. Samuel did not let anyone else hear this prophecy, so it would be up to Saul and Saul alone to one day obey this command in Gilgal. It would be the defining moment in Saul's kingdom.

IS SAUL AMONG THE PROPHETS?'
10:9-16

All of the things Samuel spoke to Saul about quickly took place, even Saul being changed by the Spirit. When he met the prophets, he began prophesying, which brought up an interesting conundrum. The people who saw Saul prophesying who knew him were amazed. They coined a phrase that would be repeated throughout the next several decades.

"Is Saul also among the prophets," was the question everyone asked. But why were the people so incredulous that Saul would prophesy? Is it that Saul was the exact opposite kind of guy who anyone would ever expect to be a holy man? Was he the last man on earth anyone would have expected God to speak to?

It seems that each time we read about Saul prophesying, the people who see it look on with disbelief and incredulity. Saul clearly had a reputation, and it probably wasn't the kind that we would be proud of.

When Saul met his uncle, Saul's servant told him they had met Samuel. Saul told his uncle about how Samuel already knew about the donkeys, but he did not say anything else about anything else. He didn't talk about the kingship, the prophecy or the word about Gilgal. Sometimes discretion is wise, but when such important decisions are on the line, it may have served Saul better to tell his uncle about Gilgal. He was going to need someone to help him remember and strengthen his hand when it came time.

SAUL PROCLAIMED KING
10:17-27

Samuel had already anointed Saul as king in a private ceremony between only the two of them. Samuel had led Israel for decades and he knew all the elders. It seems as if Samuel wanted everyone to know that Saul was God's sovereign choice for king and not his. This assembly in Mizpah was to show everyone that Samuel had not simply chosen someone he liked to be king, which would have been no different to them than his sons.

The casting of lots was a common practice in Israel, but we have little understanding of exactly how it was done. The Urim and Thummim were articles on the priests' garments, but we do not know what they looked like or how they were used. We do know that they were always used in binary questions; either for a "yes or no" or for a "this or that" answer.

Samuel casts lots, starting with Israel in general, all the way down to a single person, Saul himself. The lot actually yielded Saul as the answer without him even being visible; he had hidden himself with the supplies. At that they only knew Saul had hidden there because the Lord specifically spoke it to Samuel, apart from the lots.

Why did Saul hide? What was going on inside Saul that he would hide from everyone on the occasion of the nation finding out he was king? Was it timidity? False humility? Actual humility? Did he think the people would reject him? Was he embarrassed to take the kingdom from Samuel?

We do not know why Saul hid because our author does not tell us. We only know that this was a very odd way to start a kingdom. The Lord chose a man with remarkable physical appearance who was either ashamed or intimidated by his new position. He was caught hiding, but then was honored before the people because of his size.

When they saw Saul, almost everyone shouted "Long live the king!" The Lord would later challenge the elders' notion of what leadership looked like when another man, much larger than Saul, would challenge and terrify the nation of Israel.

Our author ends the chapter by mentioning the dissenters. There are always dissenters to every new thing, whether it is a move of the Lord or not. While everyone brought their new king gifts, the one they had asked for, some rebelled against him for one reason or another. We are told that Saul, the one hiding just moments before, took note of them, but said nothing.

Saul returned to his home in Gibeah, but now he had a posse. What was he going to do with them? In the immediate future, nothing it would seem.

1 SAMUEL CHAPTER 11

THE TERROR OF NAHASH

Saul took his band of valiant men and went back to

his father's land to tend to the profession of farming. While this may seem a noble affair for a king to so humble himself, remember that Saul was not chosen as king just to establish a monarchy. The elders of Israel had cried out to Samuel for a king for a very specific reason, and here we find out why.

According to a footnote in your Bible, Nahash, king of the Ammonites had conquered virtually all of Israel on the east side of the Jordan river. It tells us that he had gouged out the right eye of everyone living there except the seven thousand who had escaped to Jabesh Gilead.

It may be that this was removed from later copies of the text because it was found to be an exaggeration that had crept in. It may also be that this was actually very true. Regardless of the truth of the footnote, we do know that Nahash was in the process of laying siege to Jabesh. Laying siege to a walled city in ancient days was no trivial matter. It meant that an invading army would cut off all supply to and from the city and then begin building an earthen mound by which the army could simply walk over the walls with.

There was no powered earth-moving equipment then, so all this was done by hand. You can imagine that it would take a very long time, depending on how high the walls were. Some cities lay under siege for up to two years before they fell to their conquerers. We can imagine that at the very least, Jabesh had been under siege for many months. The fact that no one had saved it up to now is a black mark on Israel, but it may lend authenticity to our unpublished footnote.

If Nahash had actually conquered and abused those on the east of the Jordan as it says, it would have been a terrifying thing to oppose him. Such terror had never been heard of up to this point.

THE BARGAIN
11:1-3

When the people seeking refuge in Jabesh realized that Nahash was just days away from overtaking their city and that no one had come to their rescue yet, they decided it was time to make a bargain with him. At this point it must have seemed like the Alamo; unless they surrendered, they would all surely die.

Nahash's goals for his campaign were not based solely on military or political might. He was much less interested in expanding his territory than he was in seeing Israel disgraced. He offered the men of Jabesh to keep their lives if they came out and surrendered their right eye to him to so disgrace the nation for not standing up to him.

It further reinforces Nahash's intentions when we see that he agrees to the men of Jabesh's request to give them seven days to ask one more time for help from Israel. Nahash desperately wanted open war, not cowardly surrender. This is not your typical ancient warlording king, bent on expansion. Nahash's wicked heart was set on humiliation of his neighbors and their God.

Saul Awakened
11:4-8

Saul was anointed king by the people specifically to deal with Nahash. It must have been heart-breaking for the elders of Israel to watch their newly crowned king return home to farming instead of taking up the mandate he had been given. Saul seemed unconcerned about the fate of his fellow Israelites until one of these messengers arrived in Gibeah.

They had not even brought the message directly to Saul. He had to hear the news because he heard the weeping of the people of Gibeah. It was when he was told what was actually going on that something stirred inside him. It was at this moment that the Spirit of the Lord awakened Saul to fulfill his destiny.

It was at this point Saul "burned his bridges," so to speak. He slaughtered the oxen he was using to plow his field and sent pieces of them to all Israel, an action to alarm the people that harkened back to Judges chapter 19.

Saul began his rule by striking fear into the people of Israel, that if they did not join him in fighting against Nahash that he would instead turn his sword against them. His oath of fear worked and 330,000 men showed up at Bezek to fight against Nahash.

The Fight
11:9-11

Saul devised a ruse to lure the Ammonites into defeat. He told the men of Jabesh Gilead to tell Nahash that they would be surrendering the next day. This was intended to lead Nahash to believe that no one in Israel had come out to fight. Nahash must not have had very good spies or lookouts that Saul could hide 330,000 fighting men from him, but Saul's plan worked. It lulled the Ammonites into thinking there would be no fight.

Saul split the men up into three groups, presumably to completely surround the Ammonites, and then they completely overpowered them. Saul left no clear path for the Ammonites to retreat to, so that every single one of them had to run in a different direction.

Most battles we read about, we see how the losing party "fled along the road" to somewhere. So complete and overwhelming was Saul's victory, that no two Ammonites were left together to flee. The people must have been thinking that there had not been such a great military victory since Joshua. It deeply affected the men of Israel.

KILL THE DISSENTERS!
11:12-15

The victory was so decisive, that all the Israelites were unified around Saul as their king. It reminded them of the day of Saul's coronation and those who rejected him. They wanted their blood now since they had a powerful, victorious king.

How often men want perfect conformity! In the

midst of victory, people will call for all dissenters to be silenced. We see this even today after almost every election cycle. We see it with sports figures calling those who doubt them "haters" that will be silenced when they win. There is something about victory that flips a switch in us and causes our arrogance to run wild.

Saul, in a moment of great character, ends this talk of killing a fellow Israelite. Saul rightly devoted the victory against Nahash as a victory of the Lord, not his own strength or leadership.

Samuel was with the company Saul had called out, so he told everyone to Tavel to Gilgal to renew their kingly covenant with Saul. He had other motives behind this meeting, however.

This meeting at Gilgal was not the one Samuel had prophesied about before. That was yet to come. So why did Samuel choose Gilgal as a meeting place? Was it so Saul would remember Samuel's original prophecy? More is afoot here for Samuel than just renewing Saul's kingship.

1 Samuel Chapter 12

Have I Cheated You?
12:1-5

When the people were assembled in Gilgal, Samuel did not begin by reestablishing Saul's kingship, but by reminding them about himself. He asked them if he had defrauded them, robbed from them or taken anything from the people he shouldn't have.

The people all responded that Samuel was innocent of defrauding or oppressing anyone. This was not Samuel asking the question, but he wanted them to testify to Samuel's innocence before what the Lord was going to do before them.

Rebellion
12:6-15

Samuel gave the people a brief history lesson of how their ancestors were constantly turning away from the Lord even in the midst of supernatural salvation after salvation. The Lord performed amazing feats and "righteous acts" among the people, but still they hardened their hearts. Samuel told them of the judges God raised up to deliver the people of Israel, last of which he names as himself.

Then Samuel tells us what was truly going on behind the scenes as to why the people asked for a king. It was not because the people had rejected Samuel or his sons. It was not because they had studied the words of Moses' regarding a king and decided it was the time to ask God for a king. They did not ask God for a king because they wanted a similar deliverance like all the judges before Samuel had brought about.

No, the people asked for a king because of the terror that Nahash had allegedly struck on the east side of the Jordan and for the siege he was laying to Jabesh.

The people wanted a king specifically so they did not have to continue the cycle of sinful rejection of God, oppression by other nations and then repentance to the Lord and seeking Him for salvation. The people were not rejecting Samuel, but God.

The Israelites were tired of having to repent. They were tired of having to put away their foreign idols and gods. They wanted a king who could fight their battles and raise up an army so they could continue on in their sinful lifestyles. Before, God would only save the people when they wholeheartedly returned to Him. Their request for a king was not wicked because they wanted protection. It was wicked because they wanted protection apart from being devoted to God.

Samuel told them that was they did was wicked. He told them that if they chose to follow the Lord, and if their king did too, then the Lord would bless them. But if they turned away from the Lord, it would not be any different for them than before they had a king. The Lord was still going to send oppressors against Israel if they turned away.

The people's plan for a king who would always fight their battles was not going to work because the Lord was far too concerned with His people knowing Him to let them turn away from Him for too long. Samuel told them if they did persist in their sin, God would still fight against them and no king, no matter how strong, would save them.

THE SIGN & REPENTANCE
12:16-25

It was because Israel refused to repent and return to the Lord that they had asked for a king, but God was not content to let them continue in their sin. The Lord had shown Samuel something special was going to happen today. During the wheat harvest time of year, it rarely rained. Heavy rains in this time can be damaging to wheat or even devastating in a geography that is prone to flash-flooding.

When the people saw the thunderstorm, they were amazed. It wasn't just amazing because they had a thunderstorm during wheat harvest time, it was truly amazing because they had all heard Samuel ask the Lord for it. This was a sign of the prophet, that he could ask God to do something beyond the control of mankind, like ask for rain and thunder, and then have it happen.

When the thunderstorm came they were convicted because they realized that they were standing against a very real God who could send thunder and lightning at His prophet's command. They openly repented before the Lord, the very thing they could have done in the first place to receive the deliverance of the Lord.

Samuel told them that the Lord was not going to destroy them for their wickedness, but that they must choose to seek Him and follow Him or the Lord would bring destruction to them and Saul as well. With a king, it is not just the activity of the people that counts, but the king as well. If the king is wicked, the nation will come under discipline, and if the nation turns evil, the king would suffer too. This is a principle we see in our leaders today.

One final thing that stands out in this chapter is how seriously Samuel took his true role before the people. Samuel was truly a prophet, but it seems that his first calling was that of an intercessor. He understood that for him, it would be sinful not to pray for Israel.

What would our nations look like today if we had armies of Christians who believed it to be their God-given burden to pray for their nation and its people?

May the Lord raise up such people for us!

Don't forget to read 1 Samuel this week!
Visit 10WeekBible.com for more resources including daily podcasts, videos and more.

1 Samuel 13-15

Study Questions

1. Why did God hold Saul to such a high standard of obedience for Samuel's prophetic word?

2. Why did Israel not have any weapons besides Saul and Jonathan?

3. What do you think, was Jonathan impetuous or full of faith? Why?

Week 5 | 1 Samuel 13-15

4. Why was Jonathan victorious? How do we know when to "lay a fleece" before the Lord and when we need to act with wisdom an discernment?

5. Why did Saul make such a foolish oath? Have you ever made a foolish oath before? What happened?

6. What did God have against the Amalekites? Was He being cruel to them?

7. Why was Saul rejected as king? What did Saul do wrong?

Commentary Notes

1 Samuel Chapter 13

Saul's Rejection
13:1-14

The fact that Saul reigned over Israel longer than David did is a testimony of how true God's word was to the Israelites that He was not going to take their new king away no matter how much they asked or how badly they wanted Him to. In the history of the kings of Israel and Judah, Saul was not a bad king, but he was obviously not what the Lord intended for kingship either.

Some time had passed between the defeat of the Ammonites and what we read in chapter thirteen. Saul had time to establish a rudimentary infrastructure for a kingdom, including the resources necessary to have a standing army of 3,000 men. To pay these men as their full-time occupation would have been expensive, so Saul had obviously been collecting taxes for some time. This kind of thing does not happen overnight, which is important to remember when we think about the lag in time between Samuel's initial prophecy to Saul and now.

It does not seem that Saul had appointed his relative Abner in charge of the military yet. It seems that his military deputy at this point was Jonathan, to whom he gave command over one third of the army. Jonathan, either impetuously or under the unction of the Spirit of God, attacked a Philistine outpost at Geba nearby. This would bring about a very quick end to the détente that had existed between the two nations since Samuel had soundly defeated them nearly a generation earlier.

When Saul realized the position Jonathan had put the nation in, he quickly set about calling up all the nation for battle. Saul knew that this was the moment he needed to call the men to Gilgal for the prophesied meeting with Samuel.

The people had asked God for a king to defeat Nahash, but God said He was giving them a king because of the cries of His people against the Philistines (1 Samuel 9:16)

There is a general principal when it comes to scripture that the more clear the word is, the more difficult it will be to walk out. Another way of looking at it is the more clear a word from God is, the more you will need to know it was Him on the front end because of how difficult the circumstances will become. That was definitely true in Saul's case.

Saul had no idea how great the response of the Philistines was going to be or how scary this moment Samuel had prophesied years before would become.

The Philistines had obviously spent the generation between Samuel's victory over them and now building up a vast arsenal of military might like the world had never seen before. They had spent the fortune of their nation to buy chariots, horses, shields, armor and weapons. Now they amassed more numerously than anyone had ever heard of before.

This sent tremendous fear into the Israelites so that they started hiding in caves. They crossed the Jordan river to flee and we will be told that some even defected to save their lives. This was the greatest trouble anyone had faced during their lifetimes.

Saul waited for seven days, but on the seventh day almost no one was left with him. They were abandoning him because of the inevitable outcome they were watching unfold before their eyes. Samuel had given Saul, and Saul alone, the word about waiting seven days at Gilgal for him to offer the sacrifice. It was a word that meant nothing to anyone else there. Saul would have to stand alone on faith in the Lord that He would do what He promised through Samuel on that day years before. This was the most desperate of situations, but the Lord still required obedience from Saul.

Saul was not supposed to offer the sacrifice himself, but to wait for Samuel. This may seem trivial, but God had given such a clear direction to Saul that He required this level of obedience. This was a test for Saul, and he failed.

What perfect timing, that as soon as Saul finished offering the sacrifices, Samuel arrived! Samuel was very angry and prophesied that Saul's kingdom would end with him. He prophesied something very interesting about the king to come, David. He said that the king God had ordained to take Saul's place would be a man after the Lord's heart. What was it about David that made him a man after God's heart where Saul wasn't? What did this even mean? It is worthy studying both books of Samuel to find out.

FIGHTING WITHOUT WEAPONS
13:15-23

When Samuel rejected him, Saul took the men with him and went to his hometown. It must have been depressing when Saul counted out six hundred men to face the uncountable multitudes of Philistines. To make matters worse, they had no weapons!

How are you supposed to fight a vast army with six hundred people and two swords? How the Philistines managed to pull off the feat of keeping blacksmiths out of Israel is a mystery. Did the Philistines kill them or carry them off to Philistia? Did they employ economic sabotage by charging too far below what any blacksmith could make a living wage at in Israel? Did they cut off the supply of metal working equipment from Israel?

Whatever means they employed, it had the desired effect. All Israel was left with two swords to face to Philistia's colossal military power. Why hadn't Saul done anything about this since taking his throne? The provision for a standing defensive army was one of the sole reasons the people had asked for a king in the first place. They certainly did not get what they bargained for!

Because of this, the Philistines felt at liberty to send out raiding parties into the newly abandoned land of Israel. They would go into cities and villages and take everything of value that the Israelites had left behind when they fled before this vast army. This was a dire situation. It looked like an impending extinction of the Israelites if God did not intervene, and the prophet had left the camp and Saul alone.

If only there were someone in Israel brave enough and with enough faith in God to do something about it!

1 Samuel Chapter 14

Impetuous Jonathan
14:1-14

Saul was waiting in Gibeah for what seemed like his certain death when his son Jonathan decided he had enough with the waiting game. Again, whether impetuously or under the hand of the Holy Spirit we do not know, but we see the outcome: Jonathan struck out.

He found one of the advanced outposts of the Philistines. It was atop a mountain pass overlooking a valley below. A strategic point, the Philistines had encamped a small lookout group here to see if the Israelites had come out to fight. He conceived a plan much like Gideon's fleece to see if God was on His side.

Jonathan told his armor-bearer the plan so they would have confidence in the direction God was giving them if it went their way. If the Philistines said, "come up here," it meant the Lord was going to give them victory, but if they said, "wait there," the Lord was not with them.

The Lord answered Jonathan's fleece. The Philistines called for he and his armor bearer to come up the pass to see them. Jonathan and his armor-bearer had to literally climb up a steep embankment, hand and feet, to get to the top. The Philistines were not surprised by their assault: it was easily viewable by all of them, but when Jonathan got to the top, it was not Jonathan who was taught a lesson.

Twenty men died in the area of a good-sized American house lot. This was not a victory based on Jonathan's skill as a fighter, but because of the God he served.

Victorious Jonathan
14:15-23

The victory the Lord was providing only started with the twenty men Jonathan killed. Very soon the Philistines saw what had happened at their outpost and it struck fear into them. As they spread word throughout the camp that twenty men had died in such a small area, God troubled them even more with an earthquake. Fear in the camp quickly multiplied and the army started to flee.

Saul had men stationed high up to watch what was going on in the Philistine camp. They saw the commotion among the Philistines as it began and grew. When Saul was told something was going on, he numbered the people to find out who was gone. He must have assumed that someone had either been captured, defected or tried to make an assault by themselves. When he learned it was Jonathan who had gone, Saul must have grown worried.

Saul asked that the ark be brought to him so he could inquire of the Lord, presumably about what to do for Jonathan. It was Jonathan who had brought about this mess and now he was in trouble, or at least so Saul thought. It didn't take long before Saul realized the time for inquiring of the Lord had passed and it was time to go to battle.

It seems that everyone realized the Philistines were fleeing. From what, nobody yet knew, but the Israelites who had been captured, defected and those hiding in caves came out and joined the pursuit. This was a supernatural victory on many accounts, and one of the greatest spoils of the day for the Israelites was that they went from an army with two swords to one with as many weapons and as much armor as they could strip off the dead Philistines.

Not only did the Lord provide a great victory for the Israelites this day, He also provided for the army that their king had yet been unable to.

Foolish Oaths
14:24-30

Oaths were something very common in these days among the Israelites. They were an outward sign of integrity, honor and machismo among the manliest of men. Saul made a foolish oath in front of his men before the battle that harkens back to so many other foolish oaths.

> *And Jephthah made a vow to the Lord: "If you give the Ammonites into my hands, whatever comes out of the door of my house to meet me when I return in triumph from the Ammonites will be the Lord's, and I will sacrifice it as a burnt offering."*
>
> *Then Jephthah went over to fight the Ammonites, and the Lord gave them into his hands. He devastated twenty towns from Aroer to the vicinity of Minnith, as far as Abel Keramim. Thus Israel subdued Ammon.*
>
> *When Jephthah returned to his home in Mizpah, who should come out to meet him but his daughter, dancing to the sound of timbrels! She was an only child. Except for her he had neither son nor daughter. When he saw her, he tore his clothes and cried, "Oh no, my daughter! You have brought me down and I am devastated. I have made a vow to the Lord that I cannot break."*
>
> Judges 11:30-35

These oaths were very often horribly wicked and ill-conceived, like Jephthah's vow. The Lord was going to give Jephthah the victory, and there was no amount of bargaining with God that was going to sway Him. God was responding to the outcry of His children, not to the rash vow of the judge He had chosen and raised up.

Jesus had this to say about vows, with good reason:

> *Again, you have heard that it was said to the people long ago, 'Do not break your oath, but fulfill to the Lord the vows you have made.' But I tell you, do not swear an oath at all: either by heaven, for it is God's throne; or by the earth, for it is his footstool; or by Jerusalem, for it is the city of the Great King. And do not swear by your head, for you cannot make even one hair white or black. All you need to say is simply 'Yes' or 'No'; anything beyond this comes from the evil one.*
>
> *Matthew 5:33-37*

When you have oaths like Jephthah's and Saul's to look at, Jesus' words just sound like common sense. Saul's oath was to try and muster faith in his leadership, but demanding a fast before a battle without very specific instruction from the Lord to do so is just foolish.

The honey Jonathan ate this day in the woods was probably a very welcome shot of pure sugar adrenaline he needed after swinging a sword or two all day. The rest of the men could have used it too. Unfortunately for Jonathan, he hadn't been in the camp when his father bound everyone by oath.

What if the Israelites had eaten? What if Saul hadn't made the men take his oath? The victory that day would have been much larger, as we will see. How often do we hinder the good plans of the Lord by letting our own pride and fortune get in the way? How often do our churches and communities suffer because we make hasty oaths without waiting to hear the voice of the Lord first?

We must resist having anything to do with these kinds of things. They are not sins of passion, but of pride, jealousy and selfishness. They are premeditated and calculated, just as Saul's oath was, and they are easily avoided if we turn our ears to the voice of the Lord. We do not accidentally make foolish oaths in the same way we do not accidentally speak slander of others or gossip about ministries and people.

THE LORD SPEAKS
14:31-45

In the ancient world, the pay for volunteer warriors were the spoils of war. When victorious, those who fought would return to the camp of the losers and strip it clean of anything valuable, including livestock. In this case, the men were probably most interested in the livestock since they had not eaten anything all day. It would have been like sending all these men to the store while hungry. Everyone knows that's the number one way to come home with way too much food.

One of the earliest commands the Lord gave to mankind was that they were not allowed to eat meat with blood still in it. God made this rule as early as to Noah.

> *But you must not eat meat that has its lifeblood still in it.*
>
> *Genesis 9:4*
>
> *Do not eat any meat with the blood still in it.*
>
> *Leviticus 19:26*

The people of Israel were supposed to drain the blood from any animal before they ate it. Because Saul's men were so hungry, they decided to just eat what they could wherever they could. When Saul heard about it, he acted quickly to keep the men from sinning against the Lord. He ordered all the men to come to the stone he set up to allow them to kill their spoils and eat them properly.

It is interesting that Saul was so concerned with obedience to the Lord about this, yet not when the Lord was holding him to account. How easy it is for us to spot the wrongs and lack of faith of others, but we can be so painfully blind to our own!

After the men had eaten something, Saul wanted to continue the pursuit against the Philistines. Ahijah did not think it was wise to continue the pursuit without first asking the Lord what they should do. Even while all the men told Saul to do whatever was in his mind, the priest was the one with hesitation. What did Ahijah know that might prevent the people from being victorious?

Instead of answering Saul, the Lord remained silent. Saul was obviously not used to this, so he knew something was wrong. Was it that up to this point the Lord always spoke to Saul when he asked, or was it that he knew that as the king of the Lord's people the Lord should be answering on their behalf?

Whatever the reason, Saul decided to cast lots before the Lord to find out who was guilty of something that would cause the Lord to go silent. Saul must have been thinking of the stories he had heard of Joshua at the battle of Ai as recorded in Joshua chapter seven.

This brings up a very interesting study point. Is this a way in which the Lord still operates today, or is this kind of behavior limited to the Old Testament? We know that ever since the Holy Spirit was given on the day of Pentecost, there was no more casting lots spoken of in scripture, but the Lord did continue to speak prophetically without them. If we inquire of the Lord, should we always expect an answer like this today?

These are questions that do not seem to have a universal biblical answer. Saul must have been used to the Lord answering prophetically in these situations, so he knew there was something hindering his prayers this time. In our case today, men are certainly promised that if our relationship is not right with our wives, it will hinder our prayers:

> *Husbands, in the same way be considerate as you live with your wives, and treat them with respect as the weaker partner and as heirs with*

> *you of the gracious gift of life, so that nothing will hinder your prayers.*
>
> *1 Peter 3:7*

The general answer to whether or not there are things that hinder our prayers is yes. Specifically, it is harder to assess in every instance whether our prayers are hindered because of sin or whether the Lord is causing us to wait for answers.

> *Then Jesus told his disciples a parable to show them that they should always pray and not give up. He said: "In a certain town there was a judge who neither feared God nor cared what people thought. And there was a widow in that town who kept coming to him with the plea, 'Grant me justice against my adversary.'*
>
> *"For some time he refused. But finally he said to himself, 'Even though I don't fear God or care what people think, yet because this widow keeps bothering me, I will see that she gets justice, so that she won't eventually come and attack me!'"*
>
> *And the Lord said, "Listen to what the unjust judge says. And will not God bring about justice for his chosen ones, who cry out to him day and night? Will he keep putting them off? I tell you, he will see that they get justice, and quickly. However, when the Son of Man comes, will he find faith on the earth?"*
>
> *Luke 18:1-8*

As we grow in the Lord more and more, we can know the situations in which we absolutely should expect the Lord to speak and that if He doesn't it should cause us to ask Him why He hasn't spoken. We can never command God to speak, but we always have the grace to appeal to His kindness to speak.

In Saul's case it wasn't that the Lord spoke everything all the time, but that he knew it was in these cases the Lord always answered. Saul knew something had changed that, and for us that is an important lesson to take away. As in Saul's case, we should normally turn our attention towards ourselves if something in our relationship with the Lord changes.

It was Jonathan who had broken the oath Saul had made everyone take, but it would seem that this is a perfect time for Saul to reflect on why it was such a bad idea for him to make the oath in the first place.

The way this entire affair occurred, it seems that the Lord was more interested in chastising Saul for his rash oaths and for his pride to follow through with them. Saul had obviously not learned the lesson of Jephthah.

In the end, it was Saul's pride that was damaged more than anything else about the oath he made. He would actually have killed his own son to save face before his men, and it was his men who refused him that pride for the sake of the one who actually won the victory that day. Take note that after this, even though it was Jonathan who won the victory, that we will never again hear of him leading anyone in battle.

Saul At War
14:46-52

Saul had many flaws, but he continued to fight the battles of the Lord. The Lord gave him victory over all the enemies of Israel and He blessed Saul with a family, but sadly he replaced Jonathan as commander of troops with Abner, Saul's cousin.

1 Samuel Chapter 15

The Prophet Speaks
15:1-6

Chapter fifteen may be one of the most challenging passages in the Bible for modern readers to cope with. Why would the Lord command His people to completely wipe out, children and all, a people?

Many people approach this passage asking, "Why was God so mean to the Amalekites," when in reality our question should be, "Why was God so patient with the Amalekites?"

When the Israelites came up out of Egypt, they only needed to walk through Amalek's land. Instead of doing simply that, they went above and beyond by first asking for permission. The reward for their diplomacy was open war. The Amalekites did not fight against Israel simply because they did not like them. They brought the fight to Israel because they heard what their God had done to the Egyptians, and they wanted to preemptively avoid a similar catastrophe.

It was not because Amalek was fighting against Israel that God wanted them destroyed, it was because Amalek was trying to snuff out the God of the Israelites, the God who judged wicked nations. That brings us to the real question. If Amalek was actually fighting against God Himself, why did He let them live for so long?

The Lord allowed Amalek generations to see Israel next to them; to observe them, their way, their God and His favor and forgiveness. God was giving Amalek time to repent and turn to Him. God put Israel in close proximity to them so they could witness first hand God's goodness and authority over nature, yet generation after generation still refused to repent.

In the same way God will one day judge the earth in Revelation, He does not destroy those who sin, or we would all die a thousand deaths a year at the hand of the Lord. No, the Lord cuts off those who after many opportunities they still reject Him, His Son, His kindness and instead choose to fight against Him. The story of God's judgment in Revelation is not that He will one day judge sinners, but that He will destroy those who actually think they can fight Him and win.

That, in the same way, is where we find Amalek, and God has run out of patience for them.

VICTORY AND REJECTION
15:7-23

Samuel told Saul to completely destroy everything of the Amalekites, even the normal spoils of war. This bothered Saul, and it appears he chose not to tell the volunteer army he had amassed this one important piece of information, that they were going to fight for no pay.

When it came time to destroy everything, he backed down and allowed his men to keep the very best of the Amalekites' things, but he destroyed everything without value. He also, in the interest of international diplomacy, chose to leave Amalek's king alive—after all, those kings who show other kings mercy may one day be shown mercy themselves.

Now we see the depth of Saul's heart wandering away from the Lord. He knew that Samuel did not just hear about what happened, but that the Lord had sent him. Saul should have known that he could not hide what he did from the Lord, but still he persisted in lying to Samuel.

Saul told Samuel that he let everyone keep the best of the Amalekites' things so they could go back to Gilgal, that place where he had broken faith with God before, and sacrifice them to God. But this was a lie, and a bad one at that.

Samuel's pronouncement of God's rejection of Saul is instructive to us today. God is much more concerned with our obedience than our sacrifice. It is far more important to do the very plain and simple things the Lord has already commanded us to do than to try and offer Him something else because we do not want to obey. Is it any wonder that Jesus said that the highest expression of our love for Him will look like obedience to Him?

If you love me, keep my commands.

John 14:15

Saul's Great Weakness
15:24-35

Saul was too afraid of his men and their possible rejection of him as their leader if he did not allow them to be "paid" for their efforts in this campaign. Perhaps if he had been more clear on the front end of the campaign what the men could have expected, he could have avoided this fate? Regardless, Saul caved to the pressure for the men's time and blood not to be in vain, so he allowed them to keep what they wanted. It was only after Samuel's prophetic rejection did Saul confess to his weakness.

If that were not enough, Saul still only wanted Samuel to honor him in front of the people. Saul was less concerned with God's rejection of him as king than he was with his honor before his men. It was because of this that Samuel saw his robe-tearing as a prophetic symbol of Saul's kingdom. Even though Samuel knew that Saul had been rejected and that the Lord was going to replace him, even he gave into Saul's peer pressure.

It would seem that it was not a groveling Saul at this point that caused Samuel to accompany him, but a now scary Saul. A Saul who would kill to maintain power. A Saul who would kill even the prophet that Israel loved and listened to. We will see soon that Samuel is now also afraid of what Saul is capable of.

Before finishing with Saul and his men, Samuel did what Saul should have already done. With a pronouncement of his great wickedness, Samuel put Agag, king of the Amalekites to death before the Lord.

We must understand that this chapter is not about a vindictive, murderous God, but about a God of justice and patience. All patience that is tested for too long will eventually run out. In the same passage we see that God's patience with the Amalekites and Saul ran out in tragic convergence with each other.

Don't forget to read 1 Samuel this week!
Visit 10WeekBible.com for more resources including daily podcasts, videos and more.

1 Samuel 16-18

Study Questions

1. What was the problem with anointing David king over Israel? Why was Samuel afraid? Why were the people of Bethlehem afraid?

2. Why did Jesse make David stay away in the fields when Samuel came and commanded him to bring *all* his sons?

3. What is your opinion, why did David keep asking the same question about Goliath over and over again?

WEEK 6 | 1 SAMUEL 16-18

4. Why did God put David in Saul's court to play for him? What do you think God wanted David to learn?

5. Why did David pick up five stones on his way to meet Goliath?

6. Why did Saul become jealous of David? Did David do anything to deserve it?

7. Have you ever been on the receiving end of this kind of jealousy? Have you ever caused someone else pain because of your own jealousy?

8. Why do you think God allowed Saul to treat David this way? Why do you think God made Saul king?

COMMENTARY NOTES

1 SAMUEL CHAPTER 16

INTRODUCING DAVID
16:1-13

Samuel truly had the heart of an intercessor for his nation. Samuel was mourning over Saul as king, and the Lord almost rebukes him for the emotions he was carrying.

For Samuel, the past decade had been a very difficult time. He had to deal with the rejection of the Israelites of him as judge over them, something that had never happened before. He had to watch as the Lord intentionally gave them a bad king to illustrate how evil the intentions of their hearts were, and then he had to live through bad decision after bad decision of a leader much less capable than himself and certainly much less interested in listening to the leadership of the Lord.

In every way, Samuel suffered because of the choices the people of Israel had made. They had exchanged one of the best judges in their history for something much worse so that they could persist in their sin. So many times, people think that it is their leaders who are tearing their country apart with bad decision after bad decision. In actuality, it is more often the case that the Lord raises up bad leaders to reflect the heart condition of a nation. God gives to people what their hearts are truly longing for so that they can feel the burden and suffer under their decisions and realize how much better the Lord's ways are.

The Lord was not going to have Israel suffer forever under Saul, however, and God's grace to Samuel was that he was going to get to meet Saul's replacement before he died. The anointing of king David was premature by what may have been twenty years so that Samuel would know the Lord had picked out someone who was going to carry out the will of the Lord for Israel. There was just one problem.

Saul was still king.

For Samuel, Saul had actually changed from a timid and reluctant leader into someone who had become very comfortable with the wealth and ease of being at the top of the pile. Saul had actually become a scary man, and Samuel was convinced that if he crossed him one more time Saul would kill him. We will find out later that Samuel was not wrong.

Still, the Lord sent him to Bethlehem with an alibi. Samuel was to offer a sacrifice. Even this did not diffuse the tension. When he arrived in Bethlehem, the elders who met him there trembled. We are not told specifically why they trembled, but there are a few possible reasons.

First, Samuel had recently been the executioner on behalf of the Lord for Agag, king of Amalek. Maybe they thought Samuel was in Bethlehem to continue the capital punishment on behalf of the Lord. Another reason they may have trembled was because it was entirely possible after the embarrassment Saul had suffered under Samuel's most recent action, he had put the word out that Samuel was on thin ice. Samuel seemed to be persona non grata in Israel now because of Saul, and the elders of Bethlehem may have thought that his presence would bring Saul's wrath on them.

It may still have been also that they were intimidated by the great prophet of Israel coming to their little town. Bethlehem was small and here was the old man who could tell them all their dirty secrets, hidden from everyone but God. This is still a common fear for people today who have not settled in their hearts God's great and unending love and favor for them. Whatever the reason for their fear, Samuel arrived at Jesse's house for the business of finding a king.

The Lord had only told Samuel that one of Jesse's sons was to be king, but He did not tell him which one, or even how many he had. When Jesses paraded his sons in front of Samuel, he thought each one must have been the one. Tall, strong, handsome and each one was rejected by the Lord.

It seems trivial now that Samuel would need the Lord's correction that He looks on the heart and not on outward appearances, but our ear to the Lord does not override our propensity to be deceived by what we see. Samuel, in his age and wisdom was still swayed by what he saw instead of what the word of the Lord was. We need to ever remind ourselves of this truth: the Lord sees and judges the heart, not outward appearances, and we should always strive to align ourselves in agreement with God's judgment about people and situations.

Once all of Jesse's sons at this meeting had been presented, it left Samuel with a problem. He knew the Lord had sent him to anoint Jesse's son, but the Lord only responded negatively about each one. Was Samuel wrong about the whole affair, or was something else going on? Samuel had the presence of mind to ask Jesse, "Do you have any more sons?" We may take this for granted as we read it now, but understand the awkward moment this must have created for everyone there.

Jesse was told to bring all his sons to meet Samuel, possibly the most famous and well-respected person in Israel, and Jesse intentionally disobeyed by leaving David out. Jesse had hired hands he could have left with the sheep while David was at this meeting, so keeping David with the sheep was not a matter of convenience, but an intentional slight to young David.

Jesse had more than a handful of strong, handsome, strapping young boys, and then there was David. He was the skinny kid who enjoyed playing his guitar on the side of the hill to entertain the sheep. He was the kid who told tall tales of killing bears and lions with his bare, musical hands. To say he was different was an understatement, and it was no accident Jesse left him out.

Jesse's rebuke came as Samuel made them all stand awkwardly around in Jesse's house until David had come in from the field. The one son who was looked down upon was to be waited for while standing. Jesse and all his sons waited on pins and needles for their new king to enter the room from which he had been barred minutes before.

At the end of his life, David chose to have Israel remember him for the very thing the Lord had chosen him for in the beginning. It was not for his amazing conquests he would be remembered. It was not for the great wealth he had amassed, or the splendor of his kingdom. It was for that little beat-up lyre and his time spent worshipping the Lord with the sheep that David wanted to be remembered.

> *Now these are the last words of David. David the son of Jesse declares, The man who was raised on high declares, The anointed of the God of Jacob, And the sweet psalmist of Israel,*
>
> *2 Samuel 23:1 NASB*

David was always preeminently in his own mind a worshipper of the Lord. It was for this that the Lord chose him. God did not need another warrior, He wanted a worshipper. We were told that God had to change Saul's heart to use him. In David, the Lord said that He had instead chosen someone after His own heart and He turned Him into a warrior and king.

Let us decide in our own hearts today who we will be long before the Lord calls us to some work just as David did.

SERENDIPITY
16:14-23

This is often a troubling passage for many believers because of how it is worded. "An evil spirit from the Lord," causes grief to many, and it could be easily discounted as a translation or transliteration problem if it weren't repeated so often in the next few chapters. It bears slowing down to comprehend.

There is an idea in the church today that the Lord does not do anything negative or harmful to people. It may sound like a biblical doctrine, but in fact it is not true. The idea stems from the truth that "God is love," (1 John 4:8), therefore anything that does not look like love must not be God. To ascribe the attention of an evil spirit to God is nearly blasphemous to many modern readers.

The trouble comes in when we try to define what God's love looks like in each situation and what "negative" or "harmful" is. All too often we define how God must behave based upon how we feel He could not possibly behave rather than how scripture actually says He behaves. When we study God's Word, we must make every attempt to let it change us, not the other way around.

When the Bible says that Saul was tormented by an evil spirit from God, we must do our best to discern what it means by that than to pass it off and make excuses for why that is not what scripture means. That brings us to a difficult question: would God actually send an evil spirit to torment Saul?

The apostle Paul similarly commanded the church of Corinth to do just that:

> *So when you are assembled and I am with you in spirit, and the power of our Lord Jesus is present, hand this man over to Satan for the destruction of the flesh, so that his spirit may be saved on the day of the Lord.*
>
> 1 Corinthians 5:4-5

Knowing that the Lord would still call us to turn people over to Satan is instructive towards understanding our passage in Samuel. That fact that Paul commanded the Corinthians to turn this immoral man to Satan so that the Lord would actually redeem him is even more enlightening. God was allowing a demonic spirit to torment Saul at strategic moments to try and draw his heart back to Him.

God was also using Saul's anguish in the process to set up a meeting that was not chance.

Music is a powerful tool to connect us to our souls and the spiritual world. It can be a powerful tool to draw us closer to God, closer to our flesh or even closer to even less noble things. It was a common practice for prophets in the Old Testament to have music played while they listened to the voice of the Lord. Saul and his attendants understood the value and power of having music played to soothe his torment.

And who would they find to play for the king of all Israel but a poor, young shepherd boy living in the little town of Bethlehem? This is the powerful poetry of an Almighty God that He would bring the current yet rejected king of Israel together with the newly minted and coming king of Israel into the same room. This is a cataclysmic meeting that the Lord established to further expose the hearts of not only Saul, but all those who would be witness to what God was doing in Israel.

It would be some time before Saul would come to know who his minstrel truly was, because Samuel had taken care not to make it known what he had done in Jesse's humble home. It was due to this ignorance that Saul liked David so much and chose to make him one of his honorary armor-bearers.

1 Samuel Chapter 17

The World's Tallest Metaphor
17:1-58

The story of David and Goliath is one that is instantly familiar to nearly ever Western reader. It is a ubiquitous metaphor for every little guy facing the behemoth alone and every small endeavor challenged with a juggernaut opponent. This may be the most recognizable Old Testament narrative in the world, but we will treat it as every other passage of scripture: the Lord still wants to speak to us through it today. One of the most important aspects of hearing what God may speak today is understanding a story in its context and being able to see ourselves within the narrative.

The Israelites and the Philistines chose to face off

against each other in a valley while camping atop the hills on either side. Instead of a normal campaign where the armies met in open battle in between, the Philistines decided they would try a new tactic. They had a secret weapon they were willing to unleash on the unsuspecting Israelites. In past battles, they had scared the Israelites witless with a vast army outfitted with the most expensive wartime technology the world had ever seen. This time it would be a freak of nature no one could have dreamed up.

When the Israelite spies said there were "giants in the land" in Numbers 13, they must have been encountering Goliath's ancestors. At nearly ten feet tall, the world had never seen the likes of Goliath. His sword, shield and armor were unspeakably huge. With his helmet, Goliath may have stood over ten feet tall.

It was this man that the Philistines chose to put before Israel to taunt, tease and terrify. For forty days Goliath came out and made sport of the Israelite army, too terrified to advance and too proud to retreat. The Philistines were playing a dangerous game of chicken, having been soundly routed last time by the Israelites even after they had retreated. They did not want the same thing to happen again, so this game went on. They may have been hoping for a partial surrender from Israel just to put an end to the torment.

What the Philistines and Israel got couldn't have been further from what either were expecting.

Even though he was the newly anointed king and had been serving Israel's current king, David was still thought of as the little shepherd boy by his father and brothers. Jesse sent him to visit his older brothers with supplies for them and their commander, no doubt as a bribe for safer placement if a battle were to break out.

When David arrived at the camp on day forty, he was offended that nothing had been done about the monster they were facing. Instead of being clear and forthcoming about his intentions, David went on a very irritating campaign to make his voice heard. Eliab was annoyed by David's questioning, which was obviously not genuine interest in what would be done for the one who killed Goliath. In their argument, we see a little further into the dysfunction of Jesse's family.

Eliab's irritation was well-founded, but his accusation was not. David probably was a little conceited, but he had no intention of just watching the battle. He wanted to lead it.

David continued his disingenuous questioning until finally the right person overheard him and brought him to Saul, which was David's intention all along.

There is no consensus as to how old David was when he killed Goliath, but a few clues tell us he was probably between 18 and 21. He probably wasn't any older than 21 because of the timing and overlap of Saul's kingship with his, but he also was not a boy as so many Sunday School illustrations make him out to be. David had already been made an armor-bearer for Saul, a type of royal guard, probably not an honor held by a 13-year old.

When David stood before Saul, it was almost as if a completely new person was there. The exchange, and what was to come, make it seem as if Saul didn't even know David. It may be that in fact, he didn't. David was brought in for a simple task every so often—to play music for Saul. It is entirely possible that Saul had never had a real conversation with David up to this point and only knew David as the young man who played the lyre and was in good enough shape to be an honorary guard for him.

When Saul looked him over for this new task, he tried to talk David out of the undertaking, and that's when David's tall tales started up. We can be sure that David's brothers were sick of hearing about the lion and the bear. "Sure, David. You killed a bear today," we can hear Eliab snarking at the dinner table. The idea of David putting down his musical instrument long enough to kill a lion was just as incredulous to Shammah, but for Saul the stories were enough to convince him.

He loaded David up with his own armor, possibly the best in Israel, but David knew where his and Israel's salvation lay: not in armor or weapons, but in the hands of God Most High. David had heard the story of Jonathan taking on the Philistines with one of the only two swords in Israel. He knew of Gideon's victory and he was ready to lead Israel in their next supernatural victory.

When David went out to meet Goliath he stopped to pick up five stones from the stream. Is it coincidental

Week 6 | 1 Samuel 16-18

that Goliath had four other giant relatives that scripture tells us were later killed by David's mighty men? I think not. As he approached Goliath with his ridiculous arsenal of sticks and stones, a dialogue between what sounds like two professional wrestlers commenced.

On one side was the largest man anyone had ever seen, armed to the teeth and ready for blood. On the other side was a shepherd with a walking stick, a pouch full of stones and a homemade sling. After waiting for forty days for Israel's best, Goliath was angry that this was his challenge.

The specificity with which David verbally assaults Goliath almost makes you think that David had seen this before it happened. Had the Lord showed this scene to David in a dream sometime before? How did David know how this was going to play out as he was approaching the giant?

Notice that David did not wait for Goliath to approach him. In fact, David ran toward Goliath. So confident was David in God taking charge of the situation that he obviously felt no fear. This did not make David the bravest man in Israel, it made him the man with the greatest faith. He was that sure God was going to guide that stone.

Even after the stone sank deep into Goliath's forehead and he fell down, David didn't take any chances. He took Goliath's sword from it's sheath and ran him through a few times before the painstaking process of removing such a large head from atop the giant's shoulders. This moment is every bit as gruesome as it sounds, and all Israel and Philistia were watching. A skinny teenager had just taken down the most imposing man in human history with weapons meant to annoy vermin. What could possibly happen next?

We can be sure that it must have taken a while for the scene to set in. David may have stood there holding Goliath's head up for all to see for minutes before the Philistines could process what had just happened. Israel may have been so shocked and excited that it took them equally as long to realize the Philistines were beginning to retreat.

The Bible says that David kept Goliath's sword and armor for himself, but that he took his head to Jerusalem. Many scholars write this off as a misprint; that it meant to say to Gibeah or elsewhere. It may also be that the text is correct and that David did actually deliver the head to Jebus, the city that would later be renamed as Jerusalem. In ancient times, heads could sometimes be sent as a warning or notice that "you are next." It may have been that David was actually putting Jebus on notice that he was coming for them too. It could also mean that David held onto the head, rather morbidly, and years later set it up on display in Jerusalem.

We do not know for sure what David did with the head, but it is much more reasonable to believe the Scriptures than to try and reason away why they are incorrect. What we do know is that before delivering the head anywhere, David made sure he appeared before Saul while holding it.

Saul and Abner were incredulous that this same David, the one who played melodically for Saul, was the young man who was holding a giant's head and leading their army into battle. They knew who he was and who his father was, but they could not believe what their eyes were telling them. They had to hear it directly from his own mouth.

Our chapter ends with a most gruesome scene. Here is David standing before Abner and Saul, but instead of a harp or lyre, the bloody young man stood there holding a severed head as the hero of the day.

1 Samuel Chapter 18

David And Jonathan
18:1-4

Jonathan watched as David led the army into a most peculiar victory, one that only Jonathan himself understood. In all Israel, the only two men who had led God's people in such a supernatural victory were he and David. Jonathan was immediately joined to David in friendship, for their faith in God against all odds gave them a bond deeper than any other. Everything of sentimental value Jonathan gave to David as a seal of their covenant. When Jonathan gave David his sword, it was doubtless the very same one that he alone had on the day of the Philistine's defeat years before.

As we watch Jonathan and David's friendship grow over the years, it becomes clear that at some point Jonathan learns that David has been anointed king instead of him. It doesn't seem to bother Jonathan, but why does Jonathan never abandon his father Saul and join this man who impresses him more than anyone else? What is it that keeps Jonathan loyal to his wayward father?

THE TROUBLE BEGINS
18:5-16

As we read this chapter it may seem that all this happens immediately, but it is clear that some time passes as David's trouble unfolds. Saul was so impressed with David that he gave him men to lead in the army. He was still under the command of Abner, but David quickly grew in rank as Saul sent him out on raids.

At the same time David was making a name for himself within the army, he was becoming the stuff of legend among the Israelites too. There were no radio stations back then, so it took some time for the song someone wrote in honor of David's victory over Goliath to reach Saul's ears. When it did, everything changed. Never has a simple refrain caused so much trouble. Never has a song about victory caused so much national hardship. It was this song that would eventually lead to civil war within Israel. It would nearly get David killed in two nations.

Saul was jealous that he was only given responsibility for thousands of dead Philistines instead of David's tens-of-thousands. Saul's observation was eerily prophetic: "What more can he get than the kingdom?"

Amazingly, David and Saul resumed their original arrangement and the now great warrior David found himself playing music to soothe Saul's troubled soul again. What happens from here is nearly beyond belief.

When David began to play music for Saul, "as he usually did," he began to prophesy. It was in the midst of this atmosphere that Saul decided to murder David then and there. This spiritual mood swing is almost unbelievable. How could Saul go from tormented by evil spirits to consoled to prophesying to murderer in just a few minutes? Our author must have struggled with how to say this and eventually gave up on trying to explain it or give more detail. It just was.

Saul was unsuccessful in his attempts to kill David, but it appears that he explained away the outburst on the evil spirits that tormented him. Saul must have convinced David and everyone else that he was out of his mind when he threw the spear at David twice. How else would David have continued to serve Saul? David was used to defending himself by now and he was used to worshipping the Lord, but having to do both at the same time was probably new for David and more than just a little disconcerting.

Saul decided after this that the best thing to do was to give David a thousand men to command and send him far away. Maybe if he didn't see David anymore his jealousy and rage would subside. Unfortunately, it didn't work. David was so successful that the people began to love David far more than Saul.

IN THE FAMILY
18:17-30

At some point, Saul remembered the promise he had made about his daughter Merab to whoever killed Goliath. It occurred to him that if he made David his son-in-law he may be able to control him or use his growing fame for his own gain. It seems that Saul thought that if David was part of his family, he could task him with ever-increasing raids against the Philistines who would eventually kill him. Problem solved.

It seems that it was Saul's daughter Michal, not Merab, who wanted to marry David. David doesn't seem to honestly be principally opposed to being the king's son-in-law since he so easily gives in when Saul offered him Michal. Maybe the feelings for David that Michal had were reciprocal.

It seems that nothing in David's life was without morbidity, and the bride-price for Michal was no different. Saul asked for one hundred Philistine foreskins; yes, those foreskins, as the price for his daughter. David not only liked this idea, but he went ahead and doubled it on his own volition. Why not deliver two hundred foreskins instead of a hundred?

What Saul had intended for the undoing of David

just furthered David's fame, and now he had him in the family to contend with. Instead of putting David in the path of failure with the Philistines, David proved himself to be imminently capable.

And Israel would suffer for it.

Don't forget to read 1 Samuel this week!
Visit 10WeekBible.com for more resources including daily podcasts, videos and more.

1 Samuel 19-21

Study Questions

1. Why did Saul want David dead? Do you think Saul knew about David being anointed king at this time?

2. Why do you think Saul so quickly went back on his oath to Jonathan not to kill David?

3. What do you imagine was the thing that Samuel told David to do when they met? Why did our author leave that conversation out of this book?

4. Why did Saul expect David to show up at the feast in Gibeah after trying to kill him?

5. Why did Jonathan ask David not to kill any of his descendants? Why would he even ask to made such a strange oath?

6. Do you think Ahimelek knew why David was really at Nob?

7. What did David's lie to Ahimelek cost him? Have you ever told a lie that cost someone something you couldn't make right? How did you handle that?

8. Why do you think David took the sword of Goliath and fled to Gath?

Commentary Notes

1 Samuel Chapter 19

Striking With Force
19:1-10

Success and favor can sometimes be as much of a burden as they can a blessing. In David's case, his successes would cost him in ways he never saw coming. We can find ourselves in similar situations where other's jealousy cost us dearly. It leaves us wondering why the Lord allows those who are genuinely trying to harm us without cause to prosper and even succeed. David would write many Psalms on just such a topic.

Saul could not keep his jealousy of David internal forever and he decided it was time to put it to rest. He told Jonathan and all the rest of his attendants (who liked David) to kill him. No one acted quickly on Saul's order, which may have been because everyone was fond of David and probably more than a little scared of him. In a short time David had developed quite a reputation for being a ruthless warrior, not exactly the kind of person you wanted to "attempted murder." Fail to finish the job and he may finish you!

Jonathan took the threat so seriously that without talking to his father first, he went and warned David. David already had his suspicions, but it must have been reassuring to hear this from Jonathan. When

Jonathan did talk to Saul, it was a very disarming moment.

Saul made an oath with Jonathan that he would not kill David. It is up to our imaginations to discern whether Saul was openly lying to Jonathan at this point or if Saul actually intended to keep his oath until later reneging. Either way, this oath was certainly not going to stick. At least for the moment, David was able to come back into Saul's court and everything was as before, including David being a very effective leader.

David attacked the Philistines again and further increased the stature of his name. This was just too much for Saul to handle. After returning from battle, David was back in the palace with Saul as before, playing his lyre when an evil spirit came on Saul.

Saul had been able to explain away his murderous fits before by blaming on the evil spirit that tormented him. Things were different now. Saul, while in his right mind, had told his entire court, even his son, that David must die. Oath or not, David wasn't buying Saul's excuses any more. He realized that no demon was causing Saul to go out of his mind and try to murder David. David now knew this was premeditated.

David knew he had to escape or Saul was going to kill him at his first opportunity.

DAVID'S ESCAPE
19:11-17

Most of David's life up to this point has been nothing but success and favor. Besides the rejection of his family early on, David enjoyed the better part of a decade of honor, fame and fortune. The biggest hardship David had faced up to now was probably not ever having enough people in the room to tell his stories of victory and triumph to. God was not satisfied to let David feel the honor of victory forever.

Victory gives us confidence, but when it is all we know, it makes us arrogant. Confidence is a wonderful virtue, but it is always just a step away from a pride that can destroy. The Lord had such great plans for David that they required him to fail. They required him to know trouble. David's destiny required what was going to happen for the next several years.

Saul was determined to kill David before the next day, so he sent people to David's house, which also happened to be his own daughter's house. Michal told David he couldn't stick around, not even for a night. Michal knew her father Saul well. She testified that this was not a change in character for her father, but one that she had seen play out for years.

One of the most tragic things about this moment is not that David had to flee, or even that he left his wife behind (which is actually very sad), but that Michal was able to take one of the household idols that they kept and put it in their bed. This idol was not some little trinket that rested on a shelf in their house. It was big enough to double as David himself! Michal had not hidden this in their house, it was something they kept that they both openly knew about. How tragic that David had let this evil enter his home!

Saul's men did not try to take David by force initially because they were entering Saul's daughter's house. They were in an awkward position with a man who was mentally unstable. How were they to know if Saul would be mad at them for barging into his daughter's house without her permission? They went back to Saul empty handed. Saul's rage flared up at them, no doubt. He knew that David was not sick, but he told the men to bring him back, bed and all.

Saul actually asked Michal why she had helped her husband survive. It seems like Saul had moved into a realm of complete irrationality. He was indignant that she helped the man she loved. Her answer to her father is again helpful for us to understand this mysterious man.

Michal told Saul that David escaped and left her there saying, "Why should I kill you?" David understood that Saul's rage and jealousy against him was so great that Saul was likely to kill Michal on account of David if he caught them both together. We will soon see how right David was when Saul's rage would cause him to attempt to murder his own son.

FLEEING TO SAMUEL
19:18-24

David didn't know where to run to, so he went to the only man he thought could help him, Samuel. He was, after all, the man who had brought all this on. He had anointed David king over Israel and now David is wondering if word has leaked out. David had been very wise in keeping this a secret from Saul and everyone else, but it would seem that the loose lips of either Jesse or his brothers had begun to unravel things for him.

Our author does not record the powerful words of wisdom Samuel had for David. At such a time as this, it makes us wonder what the exchange between David and Samuel was. If only we could have been a fly on the wall in that room!

Before long, word spread that David was with Samuel, so Saul sent people to arrest David. This is where things get really fascinating. Samuel had established these schools of prophets in several locations throughout Israel. He was presiding over this one at this time, and there was a company of prophets from the school that happened to be on the road as Saul's men approached. The Spirit of the Lord was so strongly upon them that Saul's men began prophesying as they came into proximity with each other. Obviously, the men did not arrest David.

Saul decided that he would send more men, and the same thing happened again. Not to be denied the blood he so desperately desired, Saul went himself.

This time, the same thing happened to Saul, but just to make a point, the Lord came on Saul in such a way that he stripped himself naked and lay at Samuel's feet all day. God was not only humiliating Saul, but giving him one more opportunity to repent and return to Him.

Our chapter ends on a phrase we have heard before. It again points to the character and demeanor of Saul. Why was everyone so incredulous at the idea that Saul would prophesy? No one ever asked that of David. We are to understand from this that Saul just wasn't the kind of guy anyone would lump in with the likes of Samuel or the prophets.

1 Samuel Chapter 20

The Covenant
20:1-23

David realized that he was endangering Samuel by staying with him. By now Saul had found out that Samuel had anointed David as the next king of Israel and he was perfectly content killing not only David, but Samuel too. It is sad that this humiliating moment before Samuel did not change Saul's heart at all. It is as if the Lord himself had now hardened Saul's heart just as He had done with Pharaoh generations before.

> *But the Lord hardened Pharaoh's heart and he would not listen to Moses and Aaron, just as the Lord had said to Moses.*

Exodus 9:12

David knew that he had to get away from Saul, but he decided to try one last attempt at reconciliation before he fled for good. David went to Jonathan and asked him to find out why Saul wanted to kill him. Jonathan was incredulous at David's suggestion, but David knew that Saul was no longer going to divulge his plans to Jonathan about him.

The two of them hatched a plan to lie to Saul about David being absent from a feast at Saul's table. The strangest thing about this plan is not that Saul got angry that David wasn't there, but the fact that Saul actually thought he would show up in the first place! Saul had already sent men to David's house to kill him. This was now the second time both Saul and David knew that he had a premeditated plan to kill him. Why would Saul anticipate David to be there?

Jonathan knew that David had been anointed king and that David was going to inherit the kingdom of Israel instead of him. This makes it clear now why Saul is so intent on killing David. If Jonathan knew this, he probably didn't hear it from David. Word had gotten out and Saul, Jonathan and everyone else knew that Samuel had anointed David as king. This is bad for David, but in a way, it is pretty amazing that it took so long for everyone to find out.

At the feast, Saul did not think anything of David missing the first day, but when he was gone the second day he asked Jonathan where he was. Jonathan repeated the ruse he and David had constructed and Saul lost his mind. As a side note, when Saul calls Jonathan a son of a perverse and rebellious woman, some scholars believe this is because Saul's wife Ahinoam had left Saul and run away, later to marry David. This is pure speculation, but David does eventually marry a woman named Ahinoam, which is oddly coincidental, especially given how political most of David's marriages were. Our author does not ever make that connection, but it is curious why Saul calls Jonathan's mother a "perverse and rebellious" woman.

And here Saul acknowledges that he knows David had been anointed king in his place by Samuel. Saul is angry at Jonathan for betraying him and himself, aiding and abetting the man who would usurp his very throne. Saul tells Jonathan that he is only thinking of him and his coming kingdom, but when Jonathan persists in his argument, Saul tries to kill him. Saul had completely lost his mind in a blind rage.

Jonathan left and then the next day went out to carry out the secret plan he and David had hatched. It may seem odd that Jonathan and David end up meeting at the end of this encounter, begging the question why didn't they just meet in the first place to discuss what happened? Jonathan knew that if his father was intent on killing David, that he would likely have him followed because of his relationship if he left Gibeah alone. Instead, Jonathan left town for archery practice with his servant boy.

Having a witness follow him made it to where no one suspected Jonathan of anything. They probably thought Jonathan was going out to blow off steam after the angry encounter with his father. When Jonathan shouted at his servant boy that the arrows were beyond him while he was actually holding them, the servant must have thought Jonathan had lost his mind too. The boy brought the arrows back to Jonathan, and that was originally the end of Jonathan and David's plan.

When David heard Jonathan call out to the boy that the arrows were beyond him, he was supposed to run away at that moment and flee, but Jonathan could not bear it, even though they had already said their goodbyes earlier. Jonathan sent the boy away so he could meet one on one with David, a very risky encounter. What if someone had followed him and was watching from a distance or from a hiding place? Neither one of them cared because they had such a deep relationship.

David embraced Jonathan and they both wept. Our author tells us David wept the most. It must have been most difficult for David to realize that his relationship with Jonathan and everyone else in the house of Saul would not be reconciled. David was sure that Saul was intent on killing him, but the final realization was more emotional than David had expected it to be.

As they parted, Jonathan reminded David again of their oath. Jonathan knew that David would be king and wanted David's assurances that his descendants would not be killed as was common with new kingships.

1 Samuel Chapter 21

Nob
21:1-9

When David went to Nob, he had no idea what kind of trouble he was going to unleash on them. Our author foreshadows the trouble when he tells us that Ahimelek the priest trembled when he saw David.

We are not told why Ahimelek trembled, but it could be much the same as when the people of Bethlehem trembled at the sight of Samuel years earlier. Samuel had prophesied to the people that once God had given them their new king, that they would hate him more than they hated the oppression of the foreigners who were raiding their land, killing them and taking their stuff. We are never told specifically that they cried out in this way, but we see hints of it throughout Samuel, and this may be another of those cases.

One possible reason Ahimelek trembled is the fear of having any emissary from Saul show up unannounced meant bad news. By now we have seen that Saul is emotionally unstable and something of a tyrant, but it will soon get worse. Saul ruled by fear even though he was a coward when it came to facing the Philistines. Ahimelek knew Saul personally. It was him who recommended that they inquire of the Lord before further pursuing the Philistines after Jonathan's great victory, which led to Saul receiving no answer from God. Saul may have become angry with Ahimelek from that point on, and David showing up was an omen of bad news.

Another possible reason was that Ahimelek, along with much of Israel, had already heard the rumors of the rift between David and Saul. He may have, in fact, just heard from Doeg the Edomite who was presently in his company. Seeing David show up struck fear in him that Saul would pursue him there.

Regardless of the reason for Ahimelek trembling, it seems incredulous to think that Ahimelek believed David's lie. David did not travel alone. Ahimelek knew something was wrong with this picture.

David asked him for bread and Ahimelek reluctantly gave David the bread of the presence. This bread was baked daily and placed before the Lord inside the tent of Moses.

> *Make a table of acacia wood—two cubits long, a cubit wide and a cubit and a half high. Overlay it with pure gold and make a gold molding around it. Also make around it a rim a handbreadth wide and put a gold molding on the rim. Make four gold rings for the table and fasten them to the four corners, where the four legs are. The rings are to be close to the rim to hold the poles used in carrying the table. Make the poles of acacia wood, overlay them with gold and carry the table with them. And make its plates and dishes of pure gold, as well as its pitchers and bowls for the pouring out of offer-*

> ings. Put the bread of the Presence on this table to be before me at all times.
>
> *Exodus 25:23-30*

The priests alone were supposed to eat it in a holy place:

> And it shall be for Aaron and his sons, and they shall eat it in a holy place; for it is most holy to him from the offerings of the Lord made by fire, by a perpetual statute.
>
> *Leviticus 24:9*

This bread was not lawful for anyone but the priests to eat, but Ahimelek offers it to David for himself and his men so long as they have kept themselves from women. Ahimelek knows that he shouldn't be giving David the bread, but instead he chose an arbitrary requirement of ceremonial cleanliness of David. Jesus went on to honor what Ahimelek did for David even though it was not specifically allowed by the law, because he showed David mercy.

> At that time Jesus went through the grainfields on the Sabbath. His disciples were hungry and began to pick some heads of grain and eat them. When the Pharisees saw this, they said to him, "Look! Your disciples are doing what is unlawful on the Sabbath."
>
> He answered, "Haven't you read what David did when he and his companions were hungry? He entered the house of God, and he and his companions ate the consecrated bread—which was not lawful for them to do, but only for the

priests. Or haven't you read in the Law that the priests on Sabbath duty in the temple desecrate the Sabbath and yet are innocent? I tell you that something greater than the temple is here. If you had known what these words mean, 'I desire mercy, not sacrifice,' you would not have condemned the innocent. For the Son of Man is Lord of the Sabbath.

Matthew 12:1-8

Ahimelek may have known that David was lying, because David's usual men were not with him. It would be a new band of men who would quickly gather to him after this. Ahimelek probably did know, like most of Israel at this point, that David had been anointed king. Ahimelek showed David mercy when he needed it but deserved little for the amount of lying that was going on.

David made one more request of Ahimelek, which made his lie all that more apparent. He said his mission was so urgent that he did not have a weapon and he asked if the priests had any to offer. How unbelievable, yet Ahimelek offers him the one weapon they had on hand, the very sword of Goliath which David had kept as a trophy.

It is important to remember that there was truly no sword like Goliath's because of what happens next.

GATH OF ALL PLACES
21:10-15

It is hard to imagine that David could have chosen a

worse place to flee to with Goliath's sword in hand than Gath, the very town Goliath was from. Not only was Goliath from Gath, but it was also the Philistine city closest to Israel. It was likely that in all the raids and battles in which David had soundly defeated the Philistines, Gath was where David was the most recognizable.

Perhaps David thought no one would actually know what he looked like and he could go to Gath under the false pretense of being a raider who had acquired the sword from the Israelites and would gain favor with Achish by selling it back to him. Or maybe with Goliath's sword in hand he could think of no other place to flee from Saul than Gath. Whatever David's reasons for going there, they were not well thought through.

People quickly realized who he was and started talking among themselves about this man who had been sung about having killed tens of thousands of their people. When David overheard this he realized he had made a terrible mistake. He acted quickly in a most embarrassing way.

David played up the madman act so well that Achish actually bought it. At that point, he didn't care if it was David or not, he didn't want him around. Achish had David expelled from Gath and he was free to search for another hiding place, but probably without his beloved trophy of Goliath's sword.

This is one of the Bible's many stories of God saving us from our own stupidity and sin. When God has purpose for our lives, which He certainly does, there are times when even our own sin and screw-ups cannot deter Him from saving us and moving us back to where we belong, especially if our hearts are still turned toward Him. May we find ourselves in the place of David, a sinner who deeply and devoutly loves the Lord.

Don't forget to read 1 Samuel this week!
Visit 10WeekBible.com for more resources including daily podcasts, videos and more.

1 Samuel 22-24

Study Questions

1. How long do you think David could keep his new following a secret in the small cave of Adullam? Why could everyone but Saul find him?

2. Why did David leave Israel? Why did he return just because someone who claimed to be a prophet told him to?

3. Why do you think Saul thought David was coming back to Israel to kill him?

Week 8 | 1 Samuel 22-24

4. Why did David start fighting battles on behalf of the Israelites? Why do you think they were so willing to turn on him?

5. What does the Israelites willingness to turn on David tell us about the rule of king Saul?

6. Why did God prophetically tell David that He was going to give Saul into his hands to do with as he pleased?

7. Why didn't David kill Saul? Would you have killed Saul if you had this chance?

8. When do you think Saul found out about David being anointed king of Israel? Why did he ask David not to kill his descendants?

Commentary Notes

1 Samuel Chapter 22

Adullam
22:1-4

David left Gath as fast as he could. Whatever prompted him to go there in the first place now seemed like a distant, bad idea. Instead, David found a cave to hide in somewhere in the south of Judah. Adullam was somewhere about halfway between Gath and Bethlehem. This particular area is not full of caves, and the most likely contender for this cave is a small hole in the side of a hill, very difficult to find unless you knew exactly where it was.

While David was literally hiding in a hole in the ground, every undesirable man in Israel came to David. They were the people in debt who chose not to repay. They were the people who had found themselves in some kind of controversy they just wanted to escape. They were the people who were tired of the local, regional or even national leadership and thought they would go and be a part of what they thought would be the "resistance" against the government entities they hated. David did not send them away, but he also had a different plan for this band of four hundred men than to lead a rebellion against Saul.

They did not gather to David overnight. These short two verses represent a prolonged period of time that David was hiding in a cave, probably months. If the cave of Adullam is the one that most believe it to be, it would not house four hundred men, women and supplies. At some point David must have reasoned that it was only a matter of time before Saul came looking for him. If all these men and David's family had no problem finding him in the cave, it wasn't good cover anymore. David needed a new hiding place.

David decided to go visit his ancestors in Moab. He felt he had a connection with them, so he approached the king and asked if he would grant his parents safety there against Saul. David was most likely thinking that the Moabite king would not give his parents up to Saul if he asked for them, but David wasn't counting on the king double-crossing him. While we are never told what happened in the Bible, extra-biblical texts allude to the reason that David would later treat the Moabites more harshly than any other surrounding nation. For whatever reason, we are told (extra-biblically) the Moabite king killed David's parents in cold blood.

THE PROPHET
22:5

David could think of nothing better than staying away from Israel, but that's not what the Lord wanted. In his ever-growing and now army-like posse, David had a prophet named Gad. David must have had some history with Gad at this point, because without any kind of confirmation, he obeys what Gad tells him is the word of the Lord to leave Moab.

It is worth pointing out that most prophetic voices in scripture speak authoritatively as if they had always heard the voice of God in perfect clarity. This is not really the way it worked. In reality, it would have taken some time and a volume of accurate prophetic words for people to acknowledge a prophet was from the Lord. Often, prophets would declare some kind of sign ahead of time that was outside of human control. When the sign happened as they predicted, the accompanying message would be taken seriously.

Gad was one of the several prophets that David would keep company with through the years, and although we do not know their history together, we know that David took his words seriously enough that he would move his family and all his men into harm's way where Saul was trying to kill him.

DEATH & PROPHETIC FULFILLMENT AT NOB
22:6-23

When Saul heard that David had come back to Israel with a small army, he was livid. He accused all his officials of conspiring together with his son Jonathan to help David raise an army to confront him. Saul's jealousy caused him to try and murder David before, so it seems logical that Saul would see David's plans this way. If we had been wrongfully accused and had an attempted assassination made on us, we probably

Week 8 | 1 Samuel 22-24

wouldn't think twice about using our newfound army to make things right. That is not what David had in mind, but it is understandable that Saul would see it that way.

All of Saul's officials loved David and saw no reason for Saul's anger, so they were not willing to turn David in, even though it seemed obvious they could find him if they wanted to. Doeg the Edomite, seeing a great opportunity for advancement through loyalty, spoke up.

Doeg told Saul of the time months before when Ahimelek had helped David when he first fled from Saul. Saul's rage was so great that it had not subsided by the time Ahimelek had been sent for and arrived, a round-trip that would have taken at least a few hours.

Ahimelek tried to play dumb with Saul as if he did not know that David was fleeing from Saul, but Saul didn't buy it. He accused Ahimelek of helping David conspire against him. Ahimelek knew he was helping David escape, but it's impossible to know if Ahimelek was actually conspiring against Saul.

When Saul gave the order to kill Ahimelek and all his family, his men were terrified. The thought of killing a priest had never occurred to them, and just the request left them petrified. Saul quickly turned to Doeg and gave him the command, which he was more than willing to carry out. Perhaps Doeg thought that if he killed off Saul's enemies, he would be promoted to more than just a shepherd, or maybe he actually hated the Israelites and this was his opportunity to shed some enemy blood.

Whatever his reasons, Doeg carried out Saul's command with zeal. He went far beyond Saul's command and not only put to death the priests, but the entire city of Nob. He killed everything that had life in it, women, children and livestock. He carried out against the priests at Nob the command the Lord had given to Saul about the Amalekites but was unwilling to carry out.

Abiathar was the only person who escaped the tragedy that day, so he went straight to David to seek refuge. He would be faithful to David for as long as he would live after that.

1 Samuel Chapter 23

Israel's Protector
23:1-6

Saul was terrified of the Philistines. He never seemed to have any trouble attacking and defeating the other nations that surrounded Israel, but the Philistines were different. They had superior wealth. With their wealth they purchased superior military technology. Saul was a man caught up with what the eye could perceive. He struggled to trust that His God, the One True God, was greater than horses and chariots. So instead of being Israel's protector, what the people of Israel had originally asked for, he ended up being their tax collector.

When Saul heard that the people of Keilah were being attacked, his immediate response should have been to defend them. But Keilah was being attacked by the Philistines and Saul now had a palace and a full-time army to do his will. Why would he want to risk his mighty men against the Philistines for Keilah, a city of Judah, David's people?

This opened the door for David to act, and act he did. Before just attacking the Philistines to earn favor with the people of Judah, David first inquired of the Lord. The Lord made it clear through the priestly ephod Abiathar possessed, though we do not know how, that he should attack and save the people of Keilah. In a way, David was beginning to step in to his role as king and defender of Israel.

David's men pushed back against David's desire to fight for Keilah. They were already hiding from Saul and they did not see the wisdom in fighting his battles for him against a much stronger and better equipped army.

David paused and inquired of the Lord again and the Lord was gracious enough to reiterate His plan for the salvation of Keilah through David. Why the Lord allowed David the latitude to ask the same question twice where others in scripture could not is a mystery, but one thing is clear: David was teaching his men to inquire of the Lord and then to boldly carry out His will. This was not just about the spoils of war, but about fighting the Lord's battles regardless of the reward. They were learning that their hope was not in

> *Now this I know:*
> *The Lord gives victory to his anointed.*
> *He answers him from his heavenly sanctuary*
> *with the victorious power of his right hand.*
> *Some trust in chariots and some in horses,*
> *but we trust in the name of the Lord our God.*
> *They are brought to their knees and fall,*
> *but we rise up and stand firm.*
> *Lord, give victory to the king!*
> *Answer us when we call!*
>
> *Psalm 20:5-9*

their swords or gold, but in the name of the Lord their God.

WHAT HAVE YOU DONE FOR ME LATELY?
23:7-13

The Lord did give David and his men victory, but people are fickle. Once the people of Keilah realized that Saul was going to attack them on account of David, they had an easy choice. Even though David and his men had just saved them from the Philistines, they were going to be willing to give David up to Saul to save their necks.

Saul, unfortunately, was more concerned with Keilah now that David was there than when he heard about the Philistines attacking it. Instead of fulfilling his role as the military defender of Israel, he was willing to destroy a city in Israel to satisfy his jealous rage.

David not only sought the Lord when he heard about Saul coming to find him, but he again taught his men that the Lord sees everything and cares about us and our situation. David was simply willing to inquire of the Lord when Saul hadn't.

And here we see that David's band of men has now grown to about six hundred. They were a powerful force, but they did not want to face Saul and his men. When Saul found out that David had escaped from Keilah, he went back home.

SAUL'S SEARCH FOR DAVID
23:14-18

David and his very large entourage were hiding out in the desert and Saul continued looking for him. It seems like six hundred men, their wives, children and livestock in tow would be pretty easy to find, but Saul was unable. When our author tells us that Jonathan had no problem finding David, we understand more clearly what is meant by the phrase, "Day after day Saul searched for him, but God did not give David into his hands." (23:14)

Saul's inability to find and catch David was purely supernatural. David wasn't hard to find. Six hundred men had found him. Saul's own son found him. David was under the divine protection of God, something that David was going to struggle to believe the closer the Lord would let Saul get to him.

This is the last time we are told that David and

Jonathan would meet. One can only wonder why Jonathan stayed loyal to his father when he had the opportunity to join the ranks with David and escape any more attempts his father would make to end his life too. But Jonathan knew his place was with his father, even if that meant dying with him. He strengthened David with the truth that he was going to be king in Jonathan's place, and they reiterated their covenant one last time.

Sold Out
23:19-29

The people of Ziph had obviously heard about how much Saul hated David and that he was willing to destroy any city in Israel that harbored him. By this time, Saul ruled entirely by fear, and it was working on the Ziphites. They turned on David and his men faster than the people of Keilah.

Once Saul had some positive intelligence on where David was staying, he set out with a large, yet lightweight and fast-moving entourage. David and his men had their wives, children, livestock and supplies in tow with them, so they were not able to move quickly and Saul and his men were catching up quickly.

The mountains in southern Israel are rugged, but not very tall. Picture a small mountain with a ravine in between two opposing faces that come together. David and his men were running along one face of the mountain and Saul and his men were on the other.

The only reason Saul did not catch David and his men was because of the news of the Philistine attack. The most amazing thing about this story is the way the Lord set up David's deliverance.

Saul and his men were not in helicopters or Humvees, they were on foot. It took them days to get to where David was and it took the fast-footed messenger days to get to Saul. The attack on Israel by the Philistines had begun a day or two earlier and the messenger just happened to arrive at the perfect time for David. The Lord had set this all up in advance to happen at this very moment!

1 Samuel Chapter 24

The Day The Lord Spoke Of
24:1-7

Saul did not waste any time after finishing with the Philistines to turn his attention back to David. At this point, Saul's desire to kill David is beyond an obsession. He is spending precious time and money to chase David when the country is falling apart around him. He is spending the wealth of Israel providing for an army of three thousand men to kill Israel's rightful king. When strategic and covenant moments are about to happen, the enemy is always ready with a plan to undo it, but we serve a more powerful God.

Somehow, David and his men found some caves to hide in while Saul was pursuing them, which is amazing considering the size of David's force. The chase that we read about here is as exciting as any Hollywood movie. Saul serendipitously (or divinely) chose the very cave that David and his men were in to "relieve himself" in. Many people assume that Saul was defecting in the cave, but it is also possible that he was napping. Regardless of his actions, it is amazing that David was able to sneak up to Saul and cut off the corner of his robe without being noticed.

In the blink of an eye, the tables had turned and the demonized king no longer had the upper hand. He was at the mercy of David, who refused to kill him. The prophetic word that his men referred to is not recorded in the Bible, which gives us a window into David's world. In fact, we have read of many prophetic words about David either repeated or alluded to that are not found elsewhere in scripture. He was obviously used to hearing the voice of the Lord either himself or through Gad or other prophetic voices.

This word is interesting because the Lord seemed to leave the situation open-ended for David. The Lord had apparently told him that He would give Saul into his hands one day to "do with as he pleased." The Lord was testing David to see if he would exact revenge or trust in God for vengeance.

David knew that to touch Saul's life would be a sin since he was the rightful anointed king of Israel. David was sure that God would deal with him one way or another so that the simple act of cutting off a piece of Saul's robe caused David's conscience to be struck. Even though David cut off the robe for the very purpose of showing Saul he had spared his life when he had the opportunity to kill him, it still affected David deeply that he had brandished his knife in Saul's presence.

SAUL COMES TO HIS SENSES—TEMPORARILY
24:8-22

When David knew that Saul and his men were far enough away to prevent an immediate engagement, he called out after him. David was taking a calculated risk exposing himself in such a way because his men were still trapped inside the cave. If Saul had so chosen he could have ignored David's words and killed him then and there.

Saul was shocked when David pointed out that the corner of his robe was missing. A million thoughts must have flooded through his mind all at once. Memories of Goliath, a wedding, meals and military campaigns David had led must have raced through his head as he realized his son-in-law could have just killed him.

After hearing David plead his case to him, Saul responded with a contrite heart. He acknowledged that he knew that God had chosen David instead of himself or his son Jonathan, a moment of clarity we may not see again from Saul.

David was pleased to make the same covenant with Saul he had made with Jonathan not to kill off his family when the Lord established his kingdom. If only Saul's resolve to keep his word lasted as long as David's.

Don't forget to read 1 Samuel this week!
Visit 10WeekBible.com for more resources including daily podcasts, videos and more.

1 Samuel 25-27

Study Questions

1. Why do you think the death of Samuel such a small part of the narrative of 1 Samuel?

2. Why do you think David decided to provide protection for Nabal's shepherds? Should David have expected some kind of payment for his "kindness?"

3. Why did David decide to kill Nabal and every male in his household? How would you have responded?

WEEK 9 | 1 SAMUEL 25-27

4. Why do you think the Lord put Saul and his men into a deep sleep just so David could sneak into the camp to have a chance to kill him?

5. Why didn't David kill Saul this time? Would you have killed him this time?

6. Why didn't David go back to Saul this time when he swore to him he wouldn't kill him?

7. Why on earth do you think David went back to Gath??

8. What was David doing while he was staying in Ziklag and why do you think he was doing it?

COMMENTARY NOTES

1 SAMUEL CHAPTER 25

SAMUEL'S DEARTH
25:1

The death of Samuel seems like it should have garnered more than a few words in the book that bears his name, but we are given no details. The phrase "all Israel assembled and mourned for him" is a bit of hyperbole. Surely a great number of people in Israel, and probably a good representation from each tribe, gathered to mourn Samuel's passing, but every person in Israel did not show up. The obvious questions are, did David show up? Did Saul attend?

We are not told specifically that David or Saul went to the assembly, but it seems that it is Samuel's death that inspired David to move as far to the south as possible and still be in Judah. David must have reasoned that now that Samuel was dead, he had no allies left in the land of Israel who would speak on his behalf before Saul.

It seems unlikely that David would have been there, and the fact that our author does not mention Saul presiding or even attending is a bit odd, but there is no way for us to know for sure who was and wasn't there. What a sad ending for Samuel, the man who considered it a sin for him to simply not pray for Israel. He had suffered the rejection of his judgeship by the Israelites. He anointed a man in his place who was not worthy to untie his shoes and currently the man he had secretly anointed as the next king was being hunted in exile.

Our lives do not always turn out the way we think they will. Samuel was arguably the most noble and godliest of the judges in Israel's history. He was a powerful prophet who loved the Lord with all his heart, yet he was laid to rest with a broken heart over the direction the nation was going. As Christians, we can take comfort in and enjoy the benefits of this life, but we must have our hearts, minds and bodies positioned in the hope of the next life alone. Samuel's identity was not rooted in who he was in this life, but in eternity. May the same thing be said of us who love the Lord today.

NABAL
25:2-13

One of the constant problems the people of Israel faced were raids from the surrounding peoples. Imagine the fear people lived in, not knowing if and when a group of pirate raiders would enter your village or ranch and kill all the men, steal (and/or rape) your wives and children, take everything of value and burn what was left. This was the reality of those living in Israel, especially those in the outlying areas.

David and his men found a wealthy landowner in the border-lands of Israel and camped around his shepherds. David must have thought he would garner favor with a wealthy man from Judah to build some relationships within his own country. Although David had no contract in place to protect Nabal's flocks, everyone in Israel knew that David was the anointed and future rightful king of Israel. It should have been an honor for Nabal. It was unlikely that anyone was going to attack David's army of six hundred men.

When Nabal went to shear his sheep, the time when he would have sold the fleece for cash at a market or to traders, David sent his messengers to ask for anything Nabal was willing to give in return for his protection. David's request sounds like mob extortion unless you consider just how dangerous it was in those days because of the foreign raiders. Also, as the rightful king, David would one day have the right to exact taxes from everyone in Israel, so a simple request of Nabal for whatever he was willing to give does not seem excessive.

Nabal's response, on the other hand, was not like the request. Nabal alluded to the fact that he knew David had fled from Saul because he was jealous of David becoming king instead of Jonathan. He insulted David, knowing full well who he was and the anointing over his life. Nabal made a calculated bet that David would never actually be king in Saul's place.

DAVID'S RESPONSE
25:12-13

When David heard Nabal's scornful response, he

decided he had had enough. David was tired and angry. He had been driven from his home. He had lost his wife. His friends had turned on him because his father-in-law wanted him dead. His parents were living in another country and were possibly already dead because of Moab's attempt to make peace with Saul. And now the man from his own tribe who he thought would give him a little help treated him like a rebel.

In other words, David was having a bad day.

If our thoughts were exposed when someone cuts us off on the highway on a bad day, we would struggle to pass judgment on David here. David wasn't going to stand for all the dishonor anymore and he decided to start fighting for what he felt was due him. He left one third of his men with the supplies and took the other two thirds of them to kill every male in Nabal's household and ranch. Four hundred fighting men would have been an overwhelming show of force compared to whatever Nabal had.

This was not David's best day, but fortunately there was wisdom in Nabal's house.

ABIGAIL
25:14-31

One of Nabal's servants knew exactly who David was. He knew what he had been through and he knew that David was not making a humble request, but a kingly demand. When he heard Nabal's response, he was terrified of what was about to befall them, and rightly so.

It sounds like Abigail loaded up the largest round number of items she could find in their storehouse. The amount of supplies that they had on the ready speaks to just how wealthy Nabal was. Abigail acted quickly to meet David on the way before he met any of Nabal's shepherds or servants. She knew that if she waited for David to arrive at their homestead, it would be too late.

We learn from Abigail that she and all Israel did, in fact, know exactly who David was and who he would one day be. She also understood the full extent of David's plight and why he would be so angry. She pled with him to refrain from doing the wrong he had planned, not just for the sake of her household, but for the sake of David's future.

Oh, what a blessing to have others in our lives to keep us from sin when our will is too weak to fight against the enemy anymore!

DAVID FINDS A WIFE
25:32-44

Abigail's words melted David's heart as he realized just how close to disaster he had come. He knew that without her intervention, he would have killed many innocent men on account of his anger. He would not have been much different than Saul that day and he had a stranger to thank for stopping him.

Abigail wisely chose to wait until after Nabal had

sobered up to tell him about what she had done. Obviously, Nabal could have spared the provisions for David in the first place since he didn't miss them at his banquet that evening. Instead of honoring the coming king in his presence, Nabal chose to spend on himself the riches the Lord had granted him to provide for His anointed. Nabal seems like a foreshadowing of the Pharisees that would one day place themselves in the seat of king, priest and judge instead of the very Son of God.

Nabal's heart was so hard that he cared nothing about the fact that Abigail had averted a great disaster on his behalf. He was angry that she had helped that man David and as a result had a stroke or some similar medical emergency. Another ten days later and he was a dead man.

When David heard about Nabal, he thanked the Lord that he had been kept from killing Nabal and exacting his own revenge. Even though he had a terrible lapse in judgment, the Lord still kept David from executing the sin in his heart. The Lord became David's vengeance, just like He promised He would be.

When he realized that Abigail was now a widow, David must have thought to himself that he needed someone like her around at all times. What better a wife could a man have than one who would keep you from doing wrong and somehow boost your ego in the process?

Our author also mentions that David had already taken another wife named Ahinoam and that Saul had given Michal to another man in marriage. Some commentators note that Ahinoam is the same name as Saul's first wife, Jonathan's mother and that it was apparently not a common name at the time. It is curious that David married a woman by the same name after Saul had called his wife a "perverse and rebellious woman." (1 Samuel 20:30)

Had David taken Saul's first wife as retribution, as a shrewd political move, or is the name just coincidence?

1 Samuel Chapter 26

Lousy Ziphites
26:1

This was now the Zihpites second time to try and garner favor with Saul by feeding him intelligence on David's whereabouts. They should have considered the result of the first time they turned David in and changed course, but they appear to be bad predictors of winners and losers.

A Deep Sleep From The Lord
26:2-12

Saul hunted David down again, but this time David was in a better place. Less afraid to face Saul's men, it seemed that David and Saul were encamped opposite each other as if to draw up battle lines. Saul had with him three thousand of Israel's best warriors, but David had six hundred men of whom stories would one day be written about.

That night David decided to go see Saul and his camp with his own eyes. It makes us wonder if David had some prophetic foreknowledge that he would decide to go into Saul's camp from there. Our text does not tell us that David knew they were all in a deep sleep from the Lord when he set out, so how did he know he could sneak in?

Always up for some action, David's nephew Abishai volunteered to go with David into the middle of enemy territory. They walked right up to Saul and Abner, who were in the middle of the men for protection.

What did David think when he stood over Saul? What did it feel like to see the spear that had tried to pin him to the wall? How long did David stand there pondering what the Lord was doing before Abishai piped up?

Like the last time Saul was within David's authority to kill, he chose to let him live. David was not going to suffer another lapse in judgment like he had with Nabal. The Lord must have shown David in some way the opportunity he would have over Saul that night, because he seemed to prepared for this scenario. Our author knew that the camp was under the sleep of the Lord to give David another look and chance to kill Saul. What other prophetic tidbit did the Lord share with David that is not recorded here?

Spared Again
26:13-25

It was probably at morning light that David decided to make known to Saul what he had done. A safe distance away, he called out to Abner and chastised him for his failure. David knew Abner well, having served with him in the army for years. He knew he was an honorable man, for he even declared that there was no one like him, but he had failed the anointed of the Lord. Abner was dumbfounded when he noticed the spear and jug missing.

Saul knew what had happened, though. He knew it was God who had delivered him into David's hand a second time, and that David was gracious to him again. He invited David to come back to him and promised he would not harm him again. David was not stupid, because if you're doing the math, everyone has lost count now on how many times Saul had promised that.

He rebuked Saul and told him to send a young servant to retrieve his items and then David spoke, not to Saul, but to God. He shouted his prayer in the hearing of Saul, Abner and all Saul's men:

> *As surely as I valued your life today, so may the Lord value my life and deliver me from all trouble.*
>
> 1 Samuel 26:24

David and Saul went their own ways, but David determined then that he wasn't going to trust Saul ever again.

1 Samuel Chapter 27

Back to Gath?
27:1-7

The Lord had now delivered Saul into David's hands on two occasions through supernatural intervention. God had spared David's life on more occasions than that, but David didn't trust that Saul would keep to his word not to kill him. So what did David decide to do now? Of course, move to the city where he killed their giant champion. Why not move to the city that he struck with fear and the sword so that songs were written about him slaying tens of thousands of that city's inhabitants? Why not just return to the city that he had to drool and scratch at the doorpost to convince them he was crazy?

It's hard to imagine what David was thinking when he decided to go back to Gath other than being sure that it was one place Saul would never chase him.

There are, however, a different set of rules when you are a world leader. You can be the one sung about for killing thousands of enemies in battle and somehow still have amicable relations with the leader of that enemy. Somehow David managed to establish just such a relationship with Achish, King of Gath.

The last time David arrived in Gath he was alone with no company other than the sword of Goliath.

The plan wasn't terribly well thought out. This time David showed back up with six hundred of the craziest, battle-ready men, their wives, children, livestock and supplies. It must have been an odd site for the people of Gath and Achish to watch.

Imagine the procession of people and stuff that strolled through the streets of Gath. Whispers grew into shouts. "That's David! That's the one they sang about! He's the one who killed Goliath!"

It's not too often that your enemy shows up at your front door. It's even rarer when your most feared enemy shows up at the front door and asks for a place to stay, but that is exactly what David and his closest couple thousand companions did. For a while.

Achish was happy to have David in Gath because he knew that Saul wanted him dead. There's that old adage, "the enemy of my enemy is my friend." For Achish, that was perfectly exemplified here. Achish knew the longer David was with him, the less likely Saul was going to attack them. He also knew it would make David look like a traitor to his own people, so he would eventually "own" David.

David had other plans, however. After a little time had passed and he had gained Achish's trust, he asked him if he and his men could move to a country town and live there. David did not want to be inside the city walls of a fortified Philistine town, especially not with what he had planned. Achish had grown to like having David around and what better place to stage a decent-sized regiment of loyal mercenaries than outside your walls for added protection?

Achish gave David and his men the town of Ziklag, where they lived for the remainder of the year and four months we are told about.

DAVID'S TRUE PLANS
27:8-12

David had no intention of being friends with Achish. In fact, before Achish's life was over, he would end up subservient to David and then to his son Solomon. He would lose everything except his title, and he would keep that only in name. All his champions would be dead, not just Goliath, and he and his army would be decimated. Achish had no way of knowing that, but David was already planning for it.

The real reason David wanted to live outside of Gath in Ziklag was so he could carry out his raids against Israel's enemies and hide the truth from Achish. David and his men would regularly set out from Ziklag and find a group of Canaanites occupying Israeli territory and attack them. David chose those peoples who had for years and possibly centuries been raiding the southern towns of Judah, his own tribal brothers.

Whenever David attacked them, he would kill everyone. He did not let a single adult get away alive, because he did not want Achish to find out what he had been doing. In his brutality, David was trying to make a name for himself among the people of Judah to show them that he was going to be their true protector, unlike Saul who had been content with his meager palace and fighting force.

Saul stayed home even when outlying towns were attacked and plundered. David, on the other hand, was living in enemy territory and actively trying to bring down the beast from within. His brutality was to cover up for his lies. His lies concealed his true plans.

When David would return to Achish with the spoils of his raids, Achish was always impressed by the loot David had. He would ask where David had gone, and David's response was always to lie about attacking somewhere in Judah. David wanted Achish to think that he was killing his own countrymen and taking their things so that he would seem even more treacherous and treasonous to his own people. He was luring Achish into trusting him even more.

It worked. Achish began to believe that David had become so odious to his own people that he could never return.

All the while, David was plotting his return to Israel as king, and Achish was the pawn in his game.

1 Samuel 28-31

Study Questions

1. Why did Achish want David to fight Israel with him? Why did David so willingly agree?

2. Why did Saul consult a medium? Why did he ask for her to call up Samuel?

3. Do you think the Lord actually let Samuel talk to Saul? Why or why not?

Week 10 | 1 Samuel 28-31

4. Why didn't the other Philistine rulers want David fighting with them? Why was David upset he couldn't fight with them?

5. Why did David's men want to kill him when they arrived back in Ziklag?

6. What do you think it looked like for David to "strengthen himself in the Lord?"

7. Why did David send some of his plunder to people in Judah?

8. Why did the people of Jabesh Gilead risk their lives to rescue the lifeless, headless bodies of Saul and his sons?

Commentary Notes

1 Samuel Chapter 28

David's Plan Fulfilled
28:1-2

Toward the end of David's time in Philistine territory, the five regional kings of Philistia decided to launch another offensive against Israel. What better a time to do it than when their greatest warrior was not only in exile, but actually living among them!

Achish brought the news to David that they were going to be attacking Israel and that he and his men must accompany the Philistine soldiers under Achish's command. David's response was telling of his true plans.

David did not tell Achish that he would fight valiantly for him. He did not speak of his loyalty to his new Philistine compatriots or his fidelity to the Philistine cause against Israel and Saul. David said exactly what he meant, that Achish would "see what he can do," and Achish did not truly understand what David was saying. David's lies had lulled Achish into feeling safe with him. He wasn't dealing with a tame house cat in David, but a roaring, hungry lion.

Foolishly, Achish made the man who had been sung about for killing tens of thousands of his people his own personal bodyguard.

SAUL, A MEDIUM AND SAMUEL?
28:3-25

Saul heard about the approaching army of Philistines, so he mustered all the forces of Israel to counter their attack. When Saul saw their numbers, he was terrified. Saul, by himself, had never led a successful campaign against the Philistines. He was perfectly happy fighting the other neighbors of Israel, but compared to the Philistines, they were still banging rocks together. Saul felt capable of defeating Stone Age armies, but the Philistines were Iron Age warriors, and he was terrified.

In an act of false piety, possibly at the behest of, or to gain the favor of Samuel, Saul had gotten rid of all the mediums in Israel. Now that Samuel was dead and the Lord had long ago stopped speaking to him, Saul didn't know where to turn. In his desperation, he decided to track down one of these expatriated mediums. In secret, he slipped away from his troops to seek counsel.

To Saul's credit, he wasn't after just any answer from any old dead person or spirit. No, he only wanted to hear from one person. When Saul found the medium of Endor and asked for her to call up Samuel from the dead, it almost causes you to pity Saul. Here is a man of such great insecurity returning to the only voice he knew who regularly had the answers from his youth. Saul and Samuel hadn't spoken in decades now, yet here is Saul trying to communicate with him again in his greatest hour of need.

The strangest part of this story, legitimately one of the strangest stories in the Bible, is not that Saul tried to call up the dead spirit of Samuel. We have already seen that Saul did not really ever truly know the Lord. He was the one the people would speak facetiously of, "Is Saul also among the prophets?" No, the strangest part of this story is that the Lord for some reason actually allowed Samuel to be called up from the dead by a wicked medium!

Even at the sight of Samuel, a prophetic spirit came over the medium and she knew that it was actually Saul in her presence. When Samuel spoke, he reminded Saul of his failure to obey the word of the Lord. He prophesied one last time that the next day Saul and his sons would join Samuel in death.

The words caused Saul to collapse in fear. He decided to fast, possibly out of fear or possibly as a last resort to seek the face of God. Whatever his reasons, Saul was easily swayed, as always by attempts to get him to eat. After Saul had eaten rather well, he left with his men and headed back to their camp.

It is so strange that Saul went back to the battle lines with the Philistines. Maybe Saul eventually reasoned that it wasn't actually Samuel he had communicated with. Maybe he was afraid his men would think he was a coward if he didn't show back up the next day as the battle approached. Whatever his reasoning, the encounter with Samuel at the medium's house did not dissuade Saul from going back to the battle.

1 Samuel Chapter 29

Philistine Distrust of David
29:1-7

The Philistine strategy had to be based, in part, in the fact that David and his men were living among them. What better a time to launch an attack on Israel when their most feared general was in exile with them? At their board meeting of kings, or whatever they did back then, Achish must have chimed in that David was no longer a threat since he was living in Ziklag.

It must have been a shock for the other four Philistine rulers to see David and his men marching along with them to attack Israel. One could imagine the conversations going on: "Wait, Achish told us that David was with him, but we didn't think he meant he was actually coming here! Achish conveniently left that part out!"

The other rulers were very upset with Achish, because they could clearly see what David had deceived him of. They could see that there wouldn't be a better time for David to win the favor of his kingdom than to turn on the Philistines in battle and win the war for Israel.

It is one thing, strategically, to pin your hopes of military success on the backs of mercenaries. In wars throughout the ages that has yielded both positive and negative results and is always a function of who is the most desperate and who can pay the most. Soldiers for hire will always fight for the person with the most money. It is another thing entirely to fight alongside a regiment of troops from the very enemy you are attacking. David's lies had so pulled the wool over Achish's eyes that he was ready to make the greatest military mistake in history!

Fortunately for the Philistines, the other kings and commanders were not so trusting of the man of whom songs of their demise were sung. They refused to allow Achish to bring David along.

DAVID'S INTENTIONS
29:8-11

No one actually knows what was going on in David's head, but it seems that the other Philistine rulers had at least partly called out David correctly. It seemed like David must have been planning on turning on them. It is unthinkable that David would have fought against the Israelites.

Maybe David, as the Philistines said, was planning on turning on them immediately to gain Saul's favor back. This doesn't seem very likely since David had already fled to Philistine territory right after Saul promised not to kill him. What seems more likely is that David was planning on waiting for the Philistines to kill Saul for him, a possibility he had reminded Abishai of in 26:10, before turning on the Philistines. What better way to get rid of his adversary and gain the kingdom all in one fell swoop.

There was just one problem: the Lord had repeatedly reminded David that He did not want in anywhere but in Israel for years. Now here was David living for over a year in Philistine territory with his own plan to claim his throne for himself. Just because we have the promises of the Lord does not mean we understand the timing and means of the Lord. David, like Abraham, Isaac and so many others in scripture and history, had decided to take the promise of the Lord into his own hands.

In case you were wondering, it's not a good idea.

1 Samuel Chapter 30

Ziklag On Fire
30:1-6

It is unclear whether or not the Amalekites knew whose town they were raiding. Possibly they picked a town at random when they knew all the Philistines were away at war with Israel. Or maybe they specifically chose David's town when they knew he was gone as retribution for what was certainly growing rumors of David's activities. Whatever the reason, a plume of black, distressing smoke rose from Ziklag as David and his men drew closer.

Imagine as the curious looks grew into panic and then turned to hundreds of men sprinting toward their wives and children only to find everything they loved in life gone or burning. What a desperate moment!

They had faithfully followed David for years, and now this! They were promised a kingdom for themselves and their families, and now it was all gone. They had continually listened to the voices of these prophets and this madman David who was leading them in and out of danger every day. Now it seemed they were the crazy ones to have ever trusted David.

The men's weeping slowly turned into fatigue, then to anger and finally to rage. As David was mourning his own loss, he started to overhear the men talking about killing him. The fact that a group of hundreds of men with swords in hand were talking of stoning David speaks more to the reason they believed he should die more than the fact that he should die at all.

Stoning was a death reserved for blasphemers in Israel. To die by the sword was as quick and clean a death a warrior then could face. Death by a thousand stones was brutal. It was painful. It was morbid. It seems that they wanted to stone David because in that moment all the prophetic promises were instantly nullified. David went from being their hero to their false prophet, and for that he must die.

What David did next is one of the very things that makes him amazingly different, and a wonderful role model for us in our weakness.

> *…But David found strength in the Lord His God.*
>
> 1 Samuel 30:6

What exactly did David find strength in, specifically? Did he remind himself of all the times in the past that God had delivered him? Did he remind himself of the promises? Did he meditate on the written Words of God? Oh, to be a fly on the wall that day! Whatever David did, he renewed his trust in the Lord, and his men saw it.

INQUIRING OF THE LORD
30:7-8

Somehow, against all odds, David had gone from hero king to heretic blasphemer and back to hero in the course of a couple hours. When the men were ready to kill him, he sought the counsel of the Lord, and God told he and his men that they could still get everything back.

David's men knew that there was no pursuing them when they raided a town, and the treacherous treatment they and David had treated their enemies with had caused them to lose hope. But David knew that God had made promises. Promises that could not be undone because of his own poor decisions.

Unlike Saul, David was going to seek the Lord for an answer in his darkest hour instead of trying to forge ahead even when his men were against he and the Lord.

David chose to seek the Lord, and the Lord answered.

Getting Their Stuff Back
30:9-20

With the renewed hope that they could still recover everything they lost, David's men began the pursuit. Not long down the road they found an abandoned slave who knew which way the Amalekite raiding party had gone. He led David and his men to find the raiders enjoying the spoils of their easy victory.

The raiders were far greater in number than David and his men, but they were no match for them. Drunk on the spoils of raiding the part of Judah David and his men had previously provided protection to, David killed them all except for four hundred of them who escaped on camels. We do not know how many there were, but they must have been a massive regiment if the minority who escaped was the size of David's fighting force!

The Lord had protected all of David's men, their families and even their stuff! No one lost anything and in fact came back to Ziklag with more than they ever had before.

Spoils of War
30:21-31

When the four hundred men who had made the entire trip to battle met up with the other two hundred men, they were angry with them for not helping in the fight. They wanted to withhold sharing the plunder with their counterparts, but David would not hear of it. He knew that it was not their own strength that caused them to return with everything they lost and then some, but it was the grace of God.

Right then David made a rule that lasted the rest of his life. Since it was the Lord who gave victories and not the strength of his men, even the men who became tired along the way would share in the spoils of victory so long as they did not abandon their post.

When David and his men returned to Ziklag, they must have set up their tents to live in temporarily. There was so much plunder from the Amalekites that the men were all able to share in it and David still had some leftover to send as gifts to those few people in Judah who were still his friends. Everywhere David had been in the previous years that he had encountered friendly faces (probably not the Ziphites), David sent part of the plunder to buy favor and friendship.

1 Samuel Chapter 31

The Death Of Saul
31:1-6

The last few chapters our author has switched back and forth between the concurrent narratives of David and Saul. David and his men were likely still on the trip back to Ziklag when the battle between the Philistines and the Israelites began.

The battle grew fierce quickly. Our author doesn't give us any hope that the Israelites ever fared well against their adversaries. It was a slaughter before it began, just like the spirit of Samuel foretold at the medium of Endor. In anticlimactic fashion, Jonathan and two of his brothers unceremoniously died.

As they were all fleeing, an archer hit Saul. As a man of war, Saul certainly knew that he was going to die from his wound. As the Philistines drew closer, he worried what kind of horrible, unspeakable sport they would make of him if they found him alive. He begged his armor-bearer to take his life, but he was too afraid. Maybe the words of David rang in his ears, "who can lay a hand the Lord's anointed and be guiltless?" (26:9)

It is actually quite difficult to kill oneself with a sword, especially when wearing a full suit of armor. Saul's only option since his assistant refused to kill him was to place his sword against his heart and fall headfirst toward it, hoping the sword would pass quickly through him. As he watched his master die, the armor-bearer was overcome with emotion and he too fell on his own sword.

Saul met a sad, quick and tragic end. He would only be survived by one son, as we will discover. Israel was not to fare much better than him this day, either.

A Long Memory
31:7-13

Not only did Israel lose her king and his sons, but it lost most of its territory. The Israelites were so afraid without their leader that they fled and crossed over the Jordan and kept going for a while. Once the Philistines realized they had won decisively, they started going around to pick the dead clean of anything of value. The Israelites had left them an entire country of empty villages, full of stuff ripe for the taking.

When they found Saul and his sons, they took their lifeless and headless bodies and hung them from the wall of Beth Shan, an eastern-facing wall in Eastern Israel near the Jordan river. The Philistines wanted the Israelites to think twice before coming back and inhabiting the land they were just driven from. Then they took Saul's armor and put it on display in their temples to remind them of the day they won their final victory, or so they thought, against Israel and her first king.

If you recall from chapter 11, Saul's first act as king was to muster all Israel to rescue Jabesh Gilead from Nahash the Ammonite. He had terrorized Israel and the men of Jabesh were without hope unless some new judge or champion would arise to rescue them. Saul was that champion king.

Their memory was long, and in the loss of their king and his body, they crossed enemy lines, risking their lives, to retrieve the dead bodies of Saul and his sons. By the cover of night they cut them down from the wall and brought them back to Jabesh and burned them and then fasted.

Ending On A Sad Note?

And on that sad note, we end the book of 1 Samuel. Our ending doesn't have to be sad, though, because we know that Samuel wasn't written as two books, but as one. This may be the end of our study, but it is not the end of the story of the single book of Samuel. This is actually the halfway-mark, arbitrarily split to make it more consumable.

At our lowest moment in the Samuel narrative, a new champion will arise. One whom was chosen by God as a "man after My own heart." (13:14) The book is curiously named after the boy prophet at its beginning, but whose story makes up only a small portion. Samuel, however, may be a fitting name for this book. Samuel is often regarded as one of the first of the prophets of Israel, and this book is more about the prophetic awakening of the covenant of God than it is the loss of the judges or the wickedness of Saul.

At the darkest moment, but at just the right time, as Paul said, God made a way.

> *You see, at just the right time, when we were still powerless, Christ died for the ungodly.*
>
> *Romans 5:6*

As a foreshadowing of the coming Messiah, God had hand-picked a man to come and rescue Israel. Unlike David, God chose for us a man to rescue not only Israel, but all the world.

At your darkest moment, just like in this narrative of Israel, God provided for your salvation.

The story, our story, will continue in 2 Samuel.

Don't forget to read 1 Samuel this week!
Visit 10WeekBible.com for more resources including daily podcasts, videos and more.

READING CHART

WEEK 1
- ☐ Day 1: Chapters 1-5
- ☐ Day 2: Chapters 6-10
- ☐ Day 3: Chapters 11-15
- ☐ Day 4: Chapters 16-20
- ☐ Day 5: Chapters 21-25
- ☐ Day 6: Chapters 26-31

WEEK 2
- ☐ Day 1: Chapters 1-5
- ☐ Day 2: Chapters 6-10
- ☐ Day 3: Chapters 11-15
- ☐ Day 4: Chapters 16-20
- ☐ Day 5: Chapters 21-25
- ☐ Day 6: Chapters 26-31

WEEK 3
- ☐ Day 1: Chapters 1-5
- ☐ Day 2: Chapters 6-10
- ☐ Day 3: Chapters 11-15
- ☐ Day 4: Chapters 16-20
- ☐ Day 5: Chapters 21-25
- ☐ Day 6: Chapters 26-31

WEEK 4
- ☐ Day 1: Chapters 1-5
- ☐ Day 2: Chapters 6-10
- ☐ Day 3: Chapters 11-15
- ☐ Day 4: Chapters 16-20
- ☐ Day 5: Chapters 21-25
- ☐ Day 6: Chapters 26-31

WEEK 5
- ☐ Day 1: Chapters 1-5
- ☐ Day 2: Chapters 6-10
- ☐ Day 3: Chapters 11-15
- ☐ Day 4: Chapters 16-20
- ☐ Day 5: Chapters 21-25
- ☐ Day 6: Chapters 26-31

WEEK 6
- ☐ Day 1: Chapters 1-5
- ☐ Day 2: Chapters 6-10
- ☐ Day 3: Chapters 11-15
- ☐ Day 4: Chapters 16-20
- ☐ Day 5: Chapters 21-25
- ☐ Day 6: Chapters 26-31

WEEK 7
- ☐ Day 1: Chapters 1-5
- ☐ Day 2: Chapters 6-10
- ☐ Day 3: Chapters 11-15
- ☐ Day 4: Chapters 16-20
- ☐ Day 5: Chapters 21-25
- ☐ Day 6: Chapters 26-31

WEEK 8
- ☐ Day 1: Chapters 1-5
- ☐ Day 2: Chapters 6-10
- ☐ Day 3: Chapters 11-15
- ☐ Day 4: Chapters 16-20
- ☐ Day 5: Chapters 21-25
- ☐ Day 6: Chapters 26-31

WEEK 9
- ☐ Day 1: Chapters 1-5
- ☐ Day 2: Chapters 6-10
- ☐ Day 3: Chapters 11-15
- ☐ Day 4: Chapters 16-20
- ☐ Day 5: Chapters 21-25
- ☐ Day 6: Chapters 26-31

WEEK 10
- ☐ Day 1: Chapters 1-5
- ☐ Day 2: Chapters 6-10
- ☐ Day 3: Chapters 11-15
- ☐ Day 4: Chapters 16-20
- ☐ Day 5: Chapters 21-25
- ☐ Day 6: Chapters 26-31

ABOUT THE AUTHOR

Darren Hibbs is the founder of the 10 Week Bible Study. He believes that the methodology of studying the Bible in this book can radically transform your life with God.

By filling your heart and mind with the Word of God first and foremost, you will better know God's heart than if your Bible knowledge comes primarily from sermons or even the commentary provided within this book. There is nothing more powerful for transformation than a people who know for themselves the Word of God.

Darren's heart burns to bring a message of hope to a lost and broken world through the immeasurable love of Jesus. It is his heart that the church will grow in love for God and embrace His love and power so that the lost will see and hear the good news about Jesus as they see it change us.

Darren writes regularly and can be reached at
www.DarrenHibbs.com

Other Titles by 10 Week Bible

Titles in Print & Digital Formats:
1 Samuel
2 Samuel
Esther
Daniel
John
Acts
Romans
Revelation

For a full and up-to-date list of titles in print, as well as for bookstore ordering information, visit 10WeekBible.com

Find out more at 10WeekBible.com

10 Week Bible Study Podcast

If you have enjoyed this study, you may also enjoy the 10 Week Bible Study Podcast. This is a five day a week broadcast designed to help you get through each book of the Bible ten weeks at a time. It includes the reading of the entire book being studied once and helpful commentary to encourage your personal reading and study of God's Word.

You can listen to the podcast on any platform on the go or at home. For a list of easy links to subscribe to the podcast, visit 10WeekBible.com.

There, you can also subscribe to the broadcast on YouTube.

www.ingramcontent.com/pod-product-compliance
Lightning Source LLC
Chambersburg PA
CBHW070551010526
44118CB00012B/1294